The Chinchilla Care Guide

Enjoying Chinchillas as Pets

Covers: Facts, Training, Maintenance, Housing, Behavior, Sounds, Lifespan, Food, Breeding, Toys, Bedding, Cages, Dust Bath, and More

Dr Elizabeth Harding

Copyright © 2022 by Dr Elizabeth Harding

This book is copyright © protected.

No part of this book may be reproduced, stored in retrieval systems, or transmitted by any means, electronic, mechanical, photocopying, recorded or otherwise without written permission from the author or publisher.

Foreword

This book is a comprehensive guide to the care, feeding, and breeding of chinchillas. As it stands on the shelf beside your chinchilla cage it is meant to take the place of a knowledgeable chinchilla-breeding neighbor, ready to help you deal with whatever problems you might be facing.

Do note however that this book is not meant to stand in the place of medical advice, and if your Chinchilla is sick or you are in doubt about the best action to take, you should always consult your exotic animal vet.

I love the Chinchilla and I know, first hand, how difficult it is to gather the true information needed to care for them. That is the reason that I wrote this book - to show everyone how wonderful they really are.

Finally, I would like to thank the many chinchilla lovers out there. Without you this book could not have gone from being an idea, to becoming a formal book. You're a true inspiration.

Thank You

Table of Contents

Chapter One: Introduction 4

Chapter Two: What to Know Before You Buy 22

Chapter Three: Bringing Your Chinchilla Home 35

Chapter Four: Caring for a Chinchilla 50

Chapter Five: Breeding Chinchillas 83

Chapter Six: Chinchilla Maintenance 109

Chapter Seven: Common Mistakes Owners Make 130

Chapter Eight: Frequently Asked Questions 137

Appendix – Reputable Breeders 146

Index 151

Chapter One: Introduction

What is a Chinchilla?

A body like that of a mouse, fitted with a fluffy squirrel tail. A face like that of a rabbit, but with round gramophone ears. Like a guinea pig, but a thousand times cuter. What exactly is a chinchilla?

These small, round-eyed rodents come from the Andes Mountains in South America. Their fur is extremely soft—the individual hairs are up to fifty times finer than human hair—and their fur was used by the mountain-dwelling Chincha Indian tribe to make special warm, lightweight clothing. It is from this tribe that they received their name:

Chapter One: Introduction

chinchilla, means 'little chincha,' or to follow the etymology further: 'little strong one'.

Today chinchillas are increasing in popularity as exotic pets. They are mild-mannered, gentle, and wonderfully fun. They are closely related to guinea pigs.

Chinchillas require more care than guinea pigs, though, and there are some things you need to consider before making a decision to keep one.

In this book we will introduce you to this special animal, help you decide whether it is the pet for you, and, if you decide it is, give you all the information you need to take care of your chinchilla and keep it healthy and happy.

The Chinchilla in the Wild

Map 1: Chinchilla Territory Today. Light Green—*Chinchilla chinchilla*. Dark Green—*Chinchilla lanigera*

The chinchilla's original habitat is the Andes mountain country of Bolivia, Peru, and Chile, between latitudes of 32° S and 26° S. This area is semi-desert, the air is thin, and there are wide ranges in temperature. The chinchilla lives at elevations from 3,000 to 5,000 meters. The mean temperature in this area

Chapter One: Introduction

is about 16°C (60°F), but winter nights are freezing and summer days may be as warm as 40°C (104°F).

The chinchilla makes its home in rock crevices, in holes dug into the ground or under the succulent bromeliad bushes endemic to that area. They are found most often on equatorial-facing slopes and while they may live in grassland or among mountain shrubs they are most commonly found in steep, barren areas. They live in communities of up to a hundred, but that does not mean they are not territorial: on the contrary, territorial rights are very well defined and fiercely defended. A chinchilla migrating into the territory of a more dominant chinchilla would be in for a dangerous fight and might even be killed.

A chinchilla attacked will stand on its hind legs, attempting to frighten away the opposition by showing itself to be large and powerful. It will show its teeth and make ferocious barking noises, open a scent gland and release a pungent "burnt almond" odor, and if these are not effective at cowing the opposition, it will spray them with a heavy stream of urine. If this does not appear to be enough, teeth come into play and there may be a roll-and-tumble biting fight. A chinchilla has an edge over many enemies because of its thick, detachable fur; an enemy attempting to bite into a chinchilla is often left with nothing but a mouthful of hair.

Chinchillas greet each other by feeling one another with their whiskers and smelling each other, after which the older, more dominant chinchilla will often groom the younger one.

Chapter One: Introduction

While they are relatively quiet animals, they do have a wide variety of different barks, chirps, and alarm calls, which they use to communicate with each other.

Chinchillas share space not only with other chinchillas but with other small rodents as well; although they do not interbreed, the chinchilla and chinchilla rat (*Abrocoma bennetti*) may share the same nests, and the degu (*Octodon degus*) and the chinchilla share the same bushes.

During warmer days, the chinchilla stays hidden, and comes out to play in the cooler twilight. The chinchilla's diet consists primarily of plant material; leaves, twigs, bark, and occasionally seeds, although they are opportunistic and can also eat insects when they find them. They eat perched on their hind legs, using their front limbs as hands.

Chapter One: Introduction

Chinchillas produce caecotropes, half-digested droppings, and re-ingest them to extract the remaining nutrition.

A chinchilla becomes sexually mature at around twelve weeks, but a female chinchilla only becomes ready to reproduce at around eight months old. Female chinchillas are dominant and set the rules regarding sexual behavior. A mother chinchilla will have no more than two pregnancies per year, each with one or two young. The young chinchillas are called kits. They are born after 111 days of gestation and, unlike many other rodents, are born with their eyes open, a full coat of fur, and the ability to run and jump.

Father chinchillas are friendly with their offspring, and family groups are sometimes seen enjoying the sun together. A young chinchilla will suckle for eight to ten weeks, although during that time the mother will also bring

Chapter One: Introduction

her children small pieces of food and encourage them in eating explorations. Young chinchillas are very active and will play boisterously, jumping, leaping, and pirouetting. They usually lie on their backs while nursing.

Chinchillas are preyed upon on by mountain lions, foxes, snakes, hawks, and owls; and, in the past, pelt-hunters. They are very clean animals, but rather than bathe in water they roll about in volcanic dust. This dust serves to clean their fur and helps keep them warm. They will also wash their faces with their forepaws, and carefully clean out their paws with their claws. Should a chinchilla accidently get wet in a rainstorm or other accident, it would be very difficult to get dry again, as their fur is so incredibly dense. An accidental wetting can easily mean pneumonia and death.

Man and the Chinchilla

Early History

In the 1500s, when Spanish explorers began going to South America, they discovered these little creatures in the high Andes. These explorers named them after the Indian tribe which trapped and hunted them, the Chinchas, whose name appears to come from an old Inca word meaning 'strong.'

The extremely soft, warm fur of the chinchilla was introduced to Europe and became immediately popular and highly prized. But since the animals are so small, the

Chapter One: Introduction

fur of between 100 and 150 chinchillas were needed to make a single coat. Additionally, the chinchilla became hunted to near extinction.

Records show that in 1900 and 1901 a single trader, Richard Glick of Germany, dealt with 300,000 pelts (skins) alone; this was only a fraction of the chinchillas being hunted and trapped during those years. Under this enormous strain the chinchilla population was quickly decimated.

Attempts at domesticating and bringing chinchillas to Europe failed because the animals could not adapt to warm, low altitude regions or the travel conditions of the day. During several attempts, they all died during transport.

By 1910 chinchilla numbers were very much reduced, and legal protection of this little animal began as a treaty banning hunting and commercialization of chinchillas was signed by Chile, Bolivia, Argentina and Peru.

Today the chinchilla is on the critically endangered species list, and hunting is strictly prohibited. About 6,000 live at the Las Chinchillas National Reserve in Chile's Choapa Valley, which was established in 1983 especially to protect *Chinchilla lanigera*. However, although this reserve is carefully guarded and efforts are made to promote the well-being of the chinchilla, the number of wild chinchillas has been steadily decreasing rather than increasing in recent years.

Because of their low reproductive rate and the relatively long time it takes them to reach maturity, attempts to help

Chapter One: Introduction

the chinchilla recover its lost foothold in the Andes Mountains has proven to be an uphill battle.

Domestication

In 1918 an American copper miner named Mathias F. Chapman arrived in Chile and, after buying a pet chinchilla from an Indian, he became very interested in the potential of domesticating the animals and starting a lucrative fur business. He set more than twenty Indians to work for him, trapping the rodents. It was not an easy job, and the team took more than three years to trap seventeen chinchillas.

After some negotiations Chapman managed to get an export permit for eleven chinchillas from the Chilean government, and in 1922 he chose the strongest, most attractive animals—eight males and three females for the trip.

Realizing the difficulty in acclimatizing animals born in the cold, rocky Andes to other regions, he planned his journey in stages and took twelve months to bring the chinchillas down from their high altitude home to sea level. From there, they were taken by boat to California.

Chapter One: Introduction

The Japanese freighter they took was poorly ventilated and hot, and Chapman and his wife used ice-packs and wet towels placed around the cages to keep their chinchillas from getting heat stroke.

In early 1923 the party arrived in California; in spite of Chapman's careful precautions, one chinchilla had died on the trip. Two more had been born en route, bringing the count up to twelve. With these chinchillas Chapman began a highly successful fur farm, and as time went by he sold off those which had less valuable fur as specialty pets.

It is from Chapman's original eleven that most domesticated chinchillas today trace their decent.

Chinchilla Characteristics

A chinchilla may well be the softest thing you have ever touched. Every hair follicle on a chinchilla's skin contains between fifty and eighty hairs. Compare that to the one hair growing out of each follicle on your head, and you'll see why its fur is so incredibly soft. This dense coat keeps them warm in the freezing Andes weather, and is also responsible for making them prone to heat stroke in warmer climates.

Their fur is hypoallergenic and, because its density protects the skin so well, chinchillas do not develop fleas or skin parasites. The individual hairs are between 1 to 1 ½ inches long.

Chapter One: Introduction

Their fur is held loosely, though, and if you pull it, it may come off in your fingers. A frightened chinchilla has a defense mechanism known as the fur slip, whereby it releases a large section of fur when afraid or roughly handled. In the wild this mechanism meant that a predator animal, biting into a chinchilla, would be left with nothing but a mouthful of fluff when attempting to get a hold on its victim.

A chinchilla's eyes are soft and round, but underdeveloped, and they rely more on their long whiskers for information about their world. These whiskers (vibrissae) can grow up to one-third of their body length, and are used to help the chinchilla navigate both in darkness and light, and create a 'mind map' of their surroundings. As a chinchilla enters a small space or tunnel and one of its whiskers touch the wall, the other whiskers sweep the area in front of the animal to determine how much space there is to move in.

The whiskers are also used for communication between chinchillas. Long whiskers can be a sign of dominance. A chinchilla's ears are very large and sensitive, allowing them to pick up sounds from 16Hz to 125Hz. Because of this, they can be easily startled by loud noises or stressed by constant clatter.

The chinchilla's bushy tail is used for balance, and is stiff and covered with long, coarse hair. A young chinchilla's tail is very delicate and can break off if pulled or mishandled.

Chapter One: Introduction

A chinchilla's teeth are constantly growing, as much as 3-5 inches a year, and because of this they must constantly gnaw and chew on fibrous things in order to wear them away. A chinchilla is born with its teeth, and has sixteen molars and four incisors for a total of twenty teeth.

Chinchillas are crepuscular and partially nocturnal animals. They are active at night and particularly during the times of dusk and dawn. Moonlight excites them, and they may become more active when the moon is full.

Their size varies widely, but the average mature chinchilla weighs between five hundred and seven hundred grams and is about 12 inches long. That's without the big bushy tail, which can add a third again to the length. They have small forelimbs—'hands' they use for eating—and larger, well-developed back limbs. With these they can perform 'kangaroo jumps' and hop up to six feet into the air!

Chapter One: Introduction

On each of a chinchilla's four paws it has four digits, ending in delicate claws. Coarse, stiff bristles surround these claws.

Chinchillas are among the longest-living rodents, and can have a life span of over twenty years.

Chinchilla Communication and Signaling

Chinchillas have a variety of methods of communicating with each other and signaling danger. When they first meet, they feel each other with their whiskers. While grooming a younger or smaller chinchilla, a dominant chinchilla may nibble the whiskers shorter presumably to indicate dominance.

While chinchillas are often silent, they have a wide variety of vocalizations, all meaning different things. A gentle high-frequency (+600 Hz) chirruping is used especially between chinchilla mothers and their kits to signify presence and to express a happy, comfortable feeling. A shorter, gruff grunt may mean 'leave me alone, that is enough'.

A quick series of low-frequency (600 Hz) gentle grunts means "I want to contact you" or may express playful inquisitiveness. A lone male produces a "nyak, nyak" call, announcing his presence, and both male and females make low cooing sounds at breeding time.

Chapter One: Introduction

A deep, guttural snarl is made when attacking. A 'bark call', loud and harsh, is a warning of possible danger. This call is produced by the chinchilla abruptly sucking air into its nose while standing upright; it has a honking sound and is given as a sequence of three to five barks, starting abruptly and with high intensity and tapering off, and then after a brief pause beginning again.

Teeth chattering usually expresses pain or fear, although on occasion this sound is also emitted by a happy, content chinchilla in lieu of purring.

An extremely worried chinchilla will give an alarm call, a series of up to twenty very loud, high intensity squeaks. A chinchilla will also use posture to express its feelings. Standing straight with hind legs up is a sign of aggression or preparation for self-defense. Simple standing straight, still, and alert means the chinchilla is listening and questioning its environment, prepared to dash away if there is danger. Standing half-erect means it anticipates something new happening soon, and is waiting to join in it. When a chinchilla grooms itself it means it feels comfortable and relaxed. Hopping, jumping, or running about hither and thither are normal play-related behaviors and may express curiosity in the environment.

A chinchilla uses urine scenting to mark boundaries and check who has been in any given space, but the exact communication expressed with this has not been fully determined.

Chapter One: Introduction

A chinchilla is capable of learning to comprehend some human speech. In particular, a domesticated chinchilla can learn its own (1-2 syllable name) and basic words or short phrases that have been consistently repeated in a context-appropriate way, such things as no, quiet, snack, or playtime.

Different Types of Chinchillas

There are two basic types of wild chinchillas, *Chinchilla lanigera* and *Chinchilla chinchilla*. They live in different areas of the Andes. *Chinchilla lanigera* is the one most commonly kept as a pet. With a slim head shape and long tail, the light grey to brown *Chinchilla lanigera* comes from the middle ranges of the Andes Mountains.

Chinchilla chinchilla (formerly known as *Chinchilla brevicaudata*) originated in the highest, coldest parts of the Andes, and its fur is longer and denser than that of other chinchillas. It has a rounder, more compact body and a stocky appearance, and usually brown-colored.

Domesticated chinchillas are predominantly *C. lanigera* mixed with a little *Chinchilla chinchilla*. They are differentiated more by color mutations than anything else, including:

Standard gray— The basic type; grey body with white undersides. Standard gray chinchillas can be further grouped as light, medium, dark, or extra dark.

Chapter One: Introduction

Ebony—May be a glossy light gray to solid black. The ebony gene is dominant, so it can be passed down from only one parent.

Charcoal—Grey, with a matte appearance quite unlike a glossy ebony chinchilla. This gene is recessive, so a kit must receive it from both parents.

Black Velvet — Also known as Touch of Velvet (TOV)— Black from the toe to the tail, with a white underside.

Beige— Crisp white underside, beige head and back, and red eyes.

Pink White—White with pink ears and red eyes; carries the beige gene.

Mosaic—White with grey patches; a white chinchilla that carries a standard gene.

Wilson White— Pure white, with dark ears and eyes; has a dominant white gene.

Violet— Soft, dark grey color with a purplish hue; no black tipping of the fur. This gene is recessive, so only two violet parents can produce a violet offspring.

Sapphire— Soft grey with a blue hue; again, no black tipping. Another recessive gene.

Chapter One: Introduction

Differences Between Males and Females

Female chinchillas tend to be larger, 500 to 700 grams (17-25 ounces) versus the 400 to 600 grams (14-21 ounces) which is normal for males. They also tend to be more hyperactive and, at times, more aggressive. Males are calmer and some owners find them easier to tame, but they may also become protective of their cages or aggressive toward other males, and are less fond of physical play.

A female chinchilla that has been traumatized may spray urine into the face of whoever it sees as a threat. This is a defense mechanism, and will not be used toward you once your chinchilla feels safe and loved. Both males and female chinchillas can become very attached to their owners.

Chapter One: Introduction

Chinchilla Facts in Brief

- **Classification:**
- Kingdom: Animalia
- Phylum: Chordata
- Subphylum: Vertebrata
- Class: Mammalia
- Order: Rodentia
- Family: Chinchillidae
- Genus: Chinchilla

Species: *Chinchilla lanigera, Chinchilla chinchilla* (formerly *Chinchilla brevicaudata*)

Distribution in the Wild:
Previously: Chile, Bolivia, and Peru.
Today: Chile.
Habitat: Rocky mountainside, high altitude.
Social groups: Lives in large colonies with up to a hundred members.
Weight at Birth: ~35 grams (1.2 ounces).
Weight at Maturity: 400-700 grams (14-25 ounces).
Gestation Period: 111 days.
Average Age at Weaning: 60 days.
Average Age at Sexual Maturity: 240 days.
Primary Coloration: Grey with a white underside.
Diet: Primarily roots, leaves, grass, and bark; occasionally seeds, berries, or insects. They are strictly vegetarian.
Noise Level: Mostly quiet, but can vocalize in a variety of ways; barking, squeaking, chirping, or squeaking.
Temperament: Inquisitive, active, playful, but easily frightened.

Chapter One: Introduction

Lifespan: On average, 10-12 years, though some chinchillas may live for over twenty years.
Heart Rate: On average, 100 beats per minute.
Normal Body Temperature: 35.5° C to 38° C.

Chinchillas as Pets

Chinchillas are social animals and, if they have been regularly handled by humans since birth, can be friendly and affectionate. They are playful and inquisitive, lively and always moving around. They are prone to chewing up whatever they can find and are liable to poison themselves, so they do need to be kept in cages when not watched.

A single chinchilla will need lots of daily human interaction, and will come to know and love you as you spend time with it. Chinchillas need to be kept in cool, well-ventilated areas, below 70°F (22°C) and below 40 percent humidity. As they are delicate, excitable animals, they are, under most circumstances, not appropriate pets for a home with small children. However, having a new baby does not mean you need to get rid of your long-time pet! Simply make well established boundaries between your child and your chinchilla, and make sure that both have plenty of space.

Chapter Two: What To Know Before You Buy

Chapter Two: What to Know Before You Buy

How Many Should You Buy?

How many chinchilla should you start with? There is no one answer to this question. How many chinchillas are ideal for you will depend on your budget, the amount of room you have, how much time you have to spend with them and whether or not you are interested in breeding.

To begin with, chinchillas are social animals. What this means is that they enjoy the company of their own kind, and if you buy just one, you'll have to make up for whatever is lacking. A chinchilla is not one of those animals that will amuse themselves all day and night, eating,

Chapter Two: What To Know Before You Buy

sleeping, and being perfectly happy in their own little life. If you don't provide companions, you should be willing to spend a reasonable amount of time every day just playing with and interacting with your chinchilla.

If you decide to buy two, you will have fewer worries when long days of work leave you with little time to enjoy your pets, but you will need to ensure that your cage is big enough to give both of them room to run around and be their happy active selves. You will also have to monitor for fights, squabbles, or other problems that may come between your pets. If you are not interested in breeding, two males or two females tend to have fewer problems getting along than a mixed group.

However, if you are interested in having chinchilla kits down the road, go for at least one of each. However, there are a number of considerations to take into account before getting a male and female together, which are covered in the chapter on breeding.

Remember also that chinchillas are highly individualistic, so if you want more than one you may need to check for compatibility and proceed carefully with your introductions. Young chinchillas will be more open to a new cage-mate than an older one might be, but if you go about your first introductions in a sensitive manner, you can have success at any age.

For introducing either same-sex or male-female pairs use the protocol given for chinchilla introductions in the chapter on breeding.

Chapter Two: What To Know Before You Buy

Where to Buy a Chinchilla

Where should you buy your first chinchilla? The pet store, your most obvious option, is actually the most potentially problematic. There is a wide variety of temperament in chinchillas, and how friendly they are to humans depends greatly on their early conditioning.

Chinchillas in pet stores are often badly conditioned and may have been left to themselves for long times, resulting in extreme boredom that leads to fur biting (wool-pulling) and other bad habits. If you need to buy your first chinchilla from a pet-store, exercise caution.

A better option would be to buy them from a respected breeder. You can find listings of breeders in the appendix section of this book. It is recommended that you do some vetting in order to make sure that your breeder knows what they are doing and has given your chinchilla the care it needed.

Ask if the chinchilla is pedigreed, whether you can see the parents, whether the kits were handled daily (important to ensure friendliness as they grow), what the chinchillas were fed, and whether the breeder is a member of one of the major chinchilla breeders groups such as the MCBA (Mutation Chinchilla Breeders Association) or ECBC (Empress Chinchilla Breeders Cooperative) .

Another option is to buy through online classifieds or mailing lists. However, do exercise full research and caution here. There are a wide variety of reasons why

Chapter Two: What To Know Before You Buy

someone may be getting rid of a chinchilla this way, and you need to go into any deal with your eyes open to potential problems.

A seller who vets you carefully even as you vet him is likely to have treated the chinchilla you are buying well. One who will sell to the first buyer he finds is less likely to have ever cared much about his pet. Realize the chinchilla may have a history of mistreatment, and that you are unlikely to ever find out much of its history or even how old it is.

You can also often find chinchillas at Rescue Centers (UK) or your local SPCA (US). Some chinchillas in these places may be ill or traumatized by a history of mistreatment, but there are also many who were loved, cherished pets and had to be given up when their owner's circumstances changed. Remember, chinchillas live a long time. The adoption fee for these chinchillas is usually less than the cost at a pet store, and you have the added bonus of knowing you did a good deed and are giving a loving home to an otherwise 'orphaned' pet.

Chapter Two: What To Know Before You Buy

How to Choose your First Chinchilla

Owning a chinchilla is a long commitment; these little furballs can live for over a decade. Whatever issues your chinchilla brings with him or her, you will have to deal with them for a long time.

Every chinchilla is different, and so much of the future temperament and friendliness is set in place while the chinchilla is still a kit. You may want to get a young chinchilla, 12 weeks old or so. That way you two will have the greatest chance of creating a close, almost inseparable bond.

When examining your potential pet, pay attention to its general appearance. Fur chewing or patchy fur may mean that the chinchilla has been under mental strain, either through undue stresses or through boredom. Drooling

Chapter Two: What To Know Before You Buy

means that the chinchilla probably has tooth alignment problems, which is most often a terminal condition.

Look also at the eyes—they should not be pasty or watery, as this might indicate eye disease or malnutrition. Note how the animal responds to your presence or your outstretched hand; a chinchilla that has been mistreated will quickly shy away from you, and you will have an uphill battle to win its trust.

Gender labeling your chinchillas

If you plan to put two chinchillas together sometime in the future, it is very important to know which are male and which are female. It is always better to check this yourself rather than rely on what you are told: reputable pet stores have been known to label the gender of chinchillas incorrectly.

To determine whether a chinchilla is a male or a female, grasp the tail by the base and hold it up as the animal is standing on all fours. The vaginal cone and the male penis look almost identical, but a female chinchilla will have her cone and anus very close. A male will have a bit of naked skin between the penis and anus.

Can Chinchillas Be Kept With Other Pets?

Chinchillas should not be kept with other pets. Larger animals such as dogs and cats must be kept far away from

Chapter Two: What To Know Before You Buy

your chinchilla's cage, especially during the day when these nocturnal animals need their rest.

Remember, foxes, wolves, and mountain lions were some of the wild chinchilla's chief predators, and your little pet will categorize the cat stalking along the sideboard or the dog barking from the doorway as predators.

Chinchillas may be kept in the same house as other small, caged animals, but you should never allow them to share a cage with any animal other than another chinchilla. The needs and temperament of various small rodents are very different.

The fine dust of the chinchilla's dust bath may cause breathing difficulties for other small rodents, and those other animals in turn will likely prove hazardous to your chinchilla. Rabbit droppings, in particular, harbor bacteria that can easily be fatal to your chinchilla.

One possible exception may be the degu—in their original habitat, both chinchillas and degus occasionally share the same home bushes. Chinchillas sleep during the day and degus are diurnal, which means that the one is awake while the other is sleeping. However, just because this works in the wild does not mean it will work in a small, contained cage. Under contained circumstances the noise and activity level of the degus may stress the chinchilla when it is resting during the day, and the activity of the chinchilla may stress the degu at night. In some situations over-stressed chinchillas have actually killed their degu cage mate.

Chapter Two: What To Know Before You Buy

If you have a very large cage (several meters in length) and can provide careful monitoring you may experiment with placing the two animals together. In general, though, it is better to keep the species separate.

Ease and Cost of Care

A chinchilla is not a low-budget pet, whichever way you look at it. Even if you were gifted a chinchilla from a friend, there is still all the paraphernalia you need to buy; everything to make a corner of your living room as much like the Andes Mountains as possible. And then there is the possibility of vet bills which will suddenly dwarf all of those everyday costs. But if you listen to any of the many chinchilla lovers out there, the fun of having a chinchilla is definitely worth the cost and trouble.

Initial Costs

First off, you need to buy your chinchilla. For a standard gray, this is likely to cost you between $75 and $100 (£50 to £65). Other mutations will be more expensive, some as costly as $500 (£300).

For a good quality cage, expect to pay between $100 and $400 (£60-£250). Remember, you cannot put your chinchilla in a tiny mesh box like those meant for a gerbil; they need room to move about.

Chapter Two: What To Know Before You Buy

Inside the cage, you will need a minimum of; climbing ledges, bowls for eating and drinking, a wooden hut to live in, and a dust bath. Other climbing toys or such things as exercise-wheels and tunnels will help your chinchilla avoid boredom.

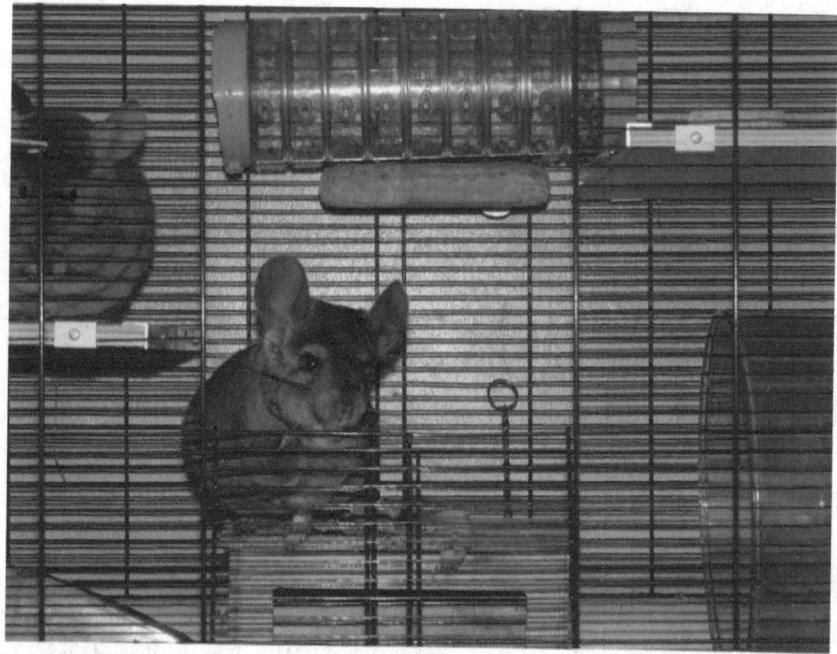

Nothing you leave in the cage should be plastic, because a chinchilla will chew on everything it can reach and plastic can be toxic.

Your basic starting out cost will look something like the following:

- Chinchilla: $75-$500 (£50 to £300)
- Cage: $100-$400 (£60-£250)
- Habitat toys and accessories: $100 (£65)

Chapter Two: What To Know Before You Buy

- Initial purchase of food & hay: $20 (£12)
- Dust for bathing: $8 (£5)
- Litter $10-$15 (£6-9)

You should also be prepared for the possibility of vet visits. A regular vet will not see chinchillas. A basic check-up with an exotic vet may cost approximately $100 (£65).

Monthly Costs

The food a chinchilla eats is not expensive—for one chinchilla, a monthly supply of alfalfa or timothy hay, supplemental food pellets and treats, litter for flooring and dust for dust baths is likely to cost you not much more than $35 (£20). That is enough of everything to last a whole month, after which you will need to go shopping again. While you can buy a few months stock, it is best not to buy more than that, for the food your chinchilla eats should always be fresh. Dust, of course, does not go stale.

Pros and Cons of owning a Chinchilla

If you have read this far, you have probably got a bit of an idea as to why one might want to buy a chinchilla. To start with, who can resist such a sweet animal?

No more lonely nights sitting in front of the television, or lying in bed counting the cracks in the ceiling. To add to this, chinchillas are so incredibly active, it is almost like getting a miniature kangaroo!

Chapter Two: What To Know Before You Buy

Moreover, a chinchilla does not have many of the negative points of other common household pets: no continuous noises, no messy droppings in hidden corners of the house, no nasty smells, and a cage to hold it when you are otherwise occupied.

However, there are some key points to consider before buying a chinchilla. For one thing, they absolutely need a cool, well-ventilated area – this is compulsory. A chinchilla will not survive at your house if it does not feel cool. They are highly sensitive to their environmental conditions. A dehumidifier unit may also be able to assist in this area.

If you have only one chinchilla, you will need to give it lots of attention, even letting it out of its cage for an hour or two every evening to run and play. At the same time, a chinchilla will get into and gnaw everything, so this free time must be supervised. It can be a fairly time consuming commitment.

Chinchillas are messy animals, and there will likely be sawdust, hay, and droppings regularly catapulted from the cage onto your floor. The cage will also need cleaning every two to three days. If this does not faze you, then it is all well and good; but if maintaining a clean cage would be too time consuming and laborious for you, then this may be a deal breaker.

The hope is that your chinchilla will not get sick, but if it does, you cannot take it to the regular vet: only vets that tend exotic animals will look at chinchillas. Therefore the

Chapter Two: What To Know Before You Buy

cost incurred could vary considerably, and may be limiting to your adoption.

Chinchillas are known to be temperamental. The one you get may be all love and friendly cuddles, or it may—and this is more likely – be the sort that says "don't touch me!" with every fiber of its being. Only buy an unknown chinchilla if you are willing to deal with the possibility of an unsociable animal, and be prepared to be loving and patient even when your advances are always repelled.

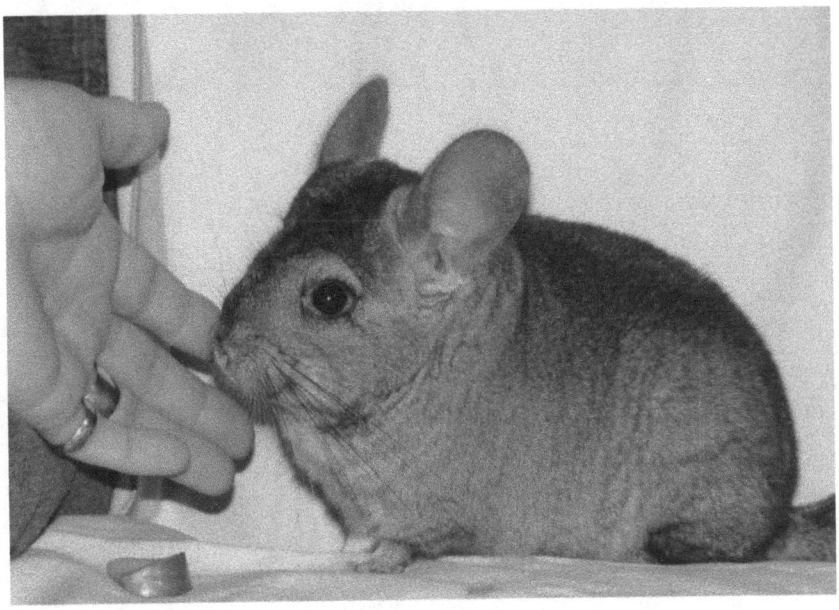

If you suffer from allergies, a chinchilla may trigger symptoms. Their fur is hypoallergenic, but the home they live in is not: they need to eat hay daily, live in sawdust, and take their baths in fine volcanic dust that have the potential to be spread around the home.

Chapter Two: What To Know Before You Buy

Also keep in mind that they sleep during the daytime—and that means they will need a quiet and peaceful place to do it in. If your home sounds like a marketplace when it doesn't sound like a playground at recess, you could struggle with keeping your chinchilla in a healthy mental state.

Chapter Three: Bringing Your Chinchilla Home

Setting Up a Home for Your Chinchilla

So you have decided to take the leap. Before you bring your chinchilla home, though, there is one more thing you need to do: prepare a home for it.

The cage you choose will be the place that your new family member will spend the greater part of its time in, and will set the stage for this entire chinchilla-adventure. If it is too small, your chinchilla will become depressed and neurotic from extreme boredom. If it is too hot, your new pet is likely to get heat stroke and could die. If it is unsafe, you are looking at a potential for ongoing vet bills—and worse. And if it is hard to clean, you will not look forward to when it is time to sanitize.

But if you choose well, it can be a pleasant, relaxing place for your chinchilla to spend its days, aesthetically pleasing, and (moderately) easy to clean.

In this chapter we will walk you through the things you need to look at when you choose your new pet's cage.

Types of Cages

First, be aware that many of the cages sold as chinchilla cages online or in popular pet stores are not appropriate.

Chapter Three: Bringing Your Chinchilla Home

There are some important things to remember while you go cage-shopping.

The first is: chinchillas move, and they move fast, so you need lots of room. The second: chinchillas eat everything. A cage with plastic parts is absolutely not appropriate for chinchillas; no matter how many times the word 'chinchilla' is printed on the box.

Your chinchilla will chew on the plastic—not the first day, perhaps, but definitely at some point when you are asleep—and can destroy the cage and poison itself.

A metal cage with plastic shelving can be used if you strip the inside and replace the plastic shelves with hard wooden shelves. Sure, the chinchilla will chew on these too, but the wood is not poisonous.

Wire shelving will hurt a chinchilla's feet and should also be replaced with wooden shelves or covered with chinchilla-safe matting. Ramps and ladders are un-necessary for chinchillas and should be taken out for safety.

The wire mesh needs to be small enough that the chinchilla cannot squeeze its head into it. Gaps should be no more than one inch, and no larger than 1 by ½ inch for a breeding cage.

Homemade Cages

If you are of a woodworking bent or if you cannot find anything that meets your chinchilla's needs, you can

Chapter Three: Bringing Your Chinchilla Home

always make a cage. You will need a sturdy design that does not use any materials which could be hazardous to chinchillas. Oak, cedar, and materials such as MDF or plywood are all off-bounds. Melamine coated pressboard is okay, as is Poly(methyl methacrylate) – also known as Plexiglas, Acrylite, Lucite, or Perspex. But you also need to be sure that there will be adequate airflow; ideally, no more than one side should be solid.

Many good designs use a sturdy wooden frame covered with wire. Neither your wood nor your mesh should be painted, coated, or polished; your chinchilla will chew off any toxic coatings within reach. The wire mesh should have holes no larger than 1 inch by 1 inch, and should be thicker than 16 gauges (approximately 1.29mm) — chicken wire will not work.

Your finished cage should also be sturdy enough to be able to stand the strain of chinchillas catapulting against it at top speeds. Multiple doors will be invaluable when the time comes for cleaning, and these doors should close and lock securely.

Make the cage tall enough to permit multiple levels or shelves and ledges, placed to allow the chinchilla to move easily from one to the other. Six or seven inches between shelves is recommended; with no jumps/drops of more than a foot horizontally or 18 inches vertically. If you intend to add large furniture like hammocks or exercise wheels later, make sure you leave room for those.

Chapter Three: Bringing Your Chinchilla Home

Make it big, and make it interesting. Your chinchilla will thank you.

A Good Cage Size

With an active animal like a chinchilla, the bigger the better. Remember the animal you are putting in this cage is not a field mouse, but an almost-kangaroo who can jump 6 feet in the air. A cage for a single chinchilla needs to be at minimum 24 inches by 15 inches and 30 inches tall, but a 3 feet by 6 feet by 6 feet tall cage would be much better. It should have multiple levels so the chinchilla can climb up and down; the sort of cages that are sold as 'high-rise,' 'mansion' or 'condo style' in pet-stores or online markets. If you cannot do levels, make sure you have some shelving.

Chapter Three: Bringing Your Chinchilla Home

A cage meant for two animals should be at least 30 by 30 by 36 inches, but preferably much bigger.

It is tricky to have more than two animals together, and keeping more than four chinchillas in one cage is generally a recipe for disaster. Chinchillas are feisty animals and can be belligerent. If you plan to have lots of animals and do breeding you will need several different cages.

Where to Position Your Cage

You need to position your cage in a cool, quiet part of the house, away from drafts, but, more importantly, away from heat. Remember your chinchilla comes from the Andes Mountains and it will not be able to cope with warm weather; its environment should be low humidity and kept stably between 55°F and 75°F (15°C-24° C).

Keep the cage away from direct sunlight, heaters, or even the air-conditioning vent, as these will introduce large fluctuations in temperature. Keep it away from bathroom, where hot water from baths and showers can bring the humidity too high.

I would highly recommend using a dehumidifier unit during the summer or cold/stormy seasons. Not only would it help keep your home free of condensation and humidity but it would really contribute towards a comfortable environment for your chinchilla.

Chapter Three: Bringing Your Chinchilla Home

Choose a place that is moderately peaceful during the daytime, when your chinchilla will be sleeping; but also where it can be 'part of family life' when it is awake in the evenings as chinchillas are not solitary animals. You also want to choose a place such that the noise they make leaping about or spinning on the exercise wheel at night will not bother anyone.

If you are a sound sleeper, that bit of space beside the desk in your bedroom may be a perfect location, but if you are a type of sleeper who awakes as soon as the wind blows a branch against the window, better choose somewhere else.

If a wire cage is set against a wallpapered wall, you are likely to wake one morning to find your chinchilla has chewed a section of the wall bare. Pay attention to everything that hangs within reach of the cage, and make sure there are no electric cords in the vicinity.

Chapter Three: Bringing Your Chinchilla Home

The floor your cage sits on should be something easy to clean: you will definitely have spills and there will be hay, sawdust, and dust to vacuum up, not to speak of messier things. If your entire house is carpeted, consider getting some plastic matting to place underneath your chinchilla's cage.

There is one more thing to take into consideration when you decide where to put your chinchilla's cage. A chinchilla should be given times of free romping outside its cage—ideally, an hour or so daily. This needs to happen in a chinchilla-proof room, and while not a necessity it will be convenient if that is the same room the cage is in, for ease of getting in and out.

Flooring for the Cage

Cages otherwise suitable for chinchillas come with two types of flooring; wire mesh or solid. Wire mesh flooring leads to sores and ulcers on a chinchilla's delicate feet as well as worse trouble when their little feet go through the wire and get stuck, so it should be avoided if possible. If you need to use a wire floor cage for whatever reason, set pieces of wood or tile down to give their feet a rest.

If the solid floor of your cage is detachable this will help greatly in cleaning; especially if it can slide out without your having to lift the entire cage.

Put a layer of wood shavings down on the floor to soak up the wetness when your chinchilla urinates. These shavings

Chapter Three: Bringing Your Chinchilla Home

should be from a wood such as aspen or kiln-dried pine. Do not use cedar or fresh pine; they will cause respiratory problems. Do not use sawdust, for the fine dust will get in your chinchillas nose, mouth, and lungs. This could prove to be very dangerous.

Litter products such as Cleanfresh are also off-limits. These products are made to absorb water by expanding, and if they are eaten, they will absorb water in the intestines and could create fatal gut blockages. Your chinchilla will taste anything within reach, so even the litter material has to be something that will not hurt it.

Alternately, you can buy or make fleece liners to put down on the floor of your cage. These should be thick and absorbent, and you change them daily, putting the soiled one in the wash as you change it for a clean one.

If you would rather not have hay, wood shavings and droppings regularly spilling from the cage onto your floor, you may also want to get guards for the bottom edges of your cage to help keep things contained.

Cage Hygiene and Care

Basic Necessities

The basic furniture in your chinchilla's cage is a wooden hutch, shelving, food and water containers and a dust bath.

Chapter Three: Bringing Your Chinchilla Home

The Hutch

The hutch should be big enough for the chinchilla to get in and be in comfortably, but small enough to feel comfy and cozy for it; ten inches each way works well. Some chinchillas will not sleep in a hutch that has only one door; if this is the case with yours, you may have to saw a back door.

Chinchilla-safe wood such as kiln-dried pine is the best material for the hutch, but cardboard boxes work too. Your chinchilla will demolish them quickly, but will enjoy doing it, and cardboard boxes are cheap and easily replaceable.

Your chinchilla should have access to plenty of hay, straw, or shredded white paper to use as nesting material. Newspaper or printed paper contains toxic inks and should not be used inside the cage.

Chapter Three: Bringing Your Chinchilla Home

Shelves

Shelves should be wooden, and placed in such a way that the chinchilla may jump from one level to another. If you have bought a cage with wire shelving it would be wise to either replace the shelves with wooden shelves or place thin boards over the wire, to avoid injury. If your cage has ramps or ladders, you should remove them.

Dust bath

The dust bath does not stay in the cage, but is put in for daily ten-minute sessions to give the chinchillas a chance to bathe. Plastic is permissible here because the chinchillas will only be using it with your direct supervision, and will be too busy enjoying the dust to be chewing. There are very convenient 'little house' models which minimize the amount of dust that is spilled or goes into the air.

Food Containers

The food dish can be wood, metal, or ceramic. It should be heavy so that it is not easily tipped. A hayrack should be well-fastened to the cage wall, and can be metal or wooden.

Water Sipper

Choose a sipper you can install on the side of your cage. Each chinchilla will need to drink around 35 ml of water per day, so make sure your bottle is large enough to provide that. The sipper tube should be metal, and must be checked regularly—several times a day, preferably—for

Chapter Three: Bringing Your Chinchilla Home

clogging. The water should be changed and the bottle and sipper tube washed with soapy water daily. Having two bottles will make this easier; that way, every day you can put in a new bottle and put the old one in the dishwasher.

If the bottle connected to the metal sipper is plastic, you can make a simple bottle guard by cutting a tin can in half lengthwise and mounting it between the bottle and cage; this way your chinchilla will not be able to reach and chew on the plastic bottle.

Additional Toys and Accessories

Toys are not optional for your chinchilla. As its teeth are constantly growing, it needs a variety of teething toys to rub them off on. Pumice stone or short lengths of apple tree wood make good chew toys.

An exercise wheel will help your chinchilla get the exercise it needs to stay healthy and to alleviate boredom. Little exercise wheels meant for hamsters and guinea pigs will not work for a chinchilla, however; choose something larger, and be sure it is not made of plastic (14 inches, or 36 cm, is a good size).

An alternate form of exercise wheel is the so-called flying saucer; some chinchillas prefer playing on this, but it takes a while to learn and some never get the hang of it.

Some chinchillas love fleece hammocks, and will even sleep on them. Others dislike the uncertain motion. You can also

Chapter Three: Bringing Your Chinchilla Home

provide your chinchilla with fleece tubes to climb into or even fleece hidey-houses.

A granite or marble tile set on the floor or somewhere else in your chinchilla's cage can give it a cool place to stand when the air temperature begins to be uncomfortably warm. If you set it on a shelf make sure it is stable and the chinchilla cannot knock it off.

Homemade Toys and Accessories

You can add something of your own by making handmade toys and cage accessories for your chinchilla. The main thing to remember is that they will be eaten, and so they need to be made out of non-toxic material, with no paints or glazes.

Some wood is also toxic to chinchillas, so be careful which you choose. Apple, mulberry, pear, willow, or hazelnut wood are all safe for your chinchilla. Cherry, plum, walnut, cedar, fresh pine, or citrus woods such as orange or lemon all have the potential to poison.

If you are collecting your own wood for your chinchilla you should give it a pretreatment to kill any micro-organisms or insects. First scrub the wood with a brush while running water over it, then shake it dry and put it in the oven to pasteurize it. If you are doing a lot at once, group similar sized pieces together on baking sheets as they will have similar cooking times. Bake at your oven's lowest setting until the wood is nicely dried out; a little over an hour for

Chapter Three: Bringing Your Chinchilla Home

most medium sized pieces. Take it out and let it cool before putting it away or giving it to your chinchilla for a teething toy.

If you want to give your chinchilla soft toys for cuddling or hammocks, pillows, soft tubes, and hidey houses you can make them out of non-piling fleece. Fleece is good for chinchillas because it does not unravel when chewed. Just make sure all loose strings from your sewing are well stowed away and use hidden stitching where practical.

Making Your Cage Homey and Comfortable

Chapter Three: Bringing Your Chinchilla Home

When preparing your chinchilla's cage, put yourself in its place. You are a rodent from the Andes Mountains. You like to burrow under rock piles or play under bushes, and sometimes you like to climb the rock piles and sit on the top of big boulders in the light of the moon. You enjoy running and dancing and leaping high in the air. You enjoy gnawing everything around you, and everything around you is gnaw-able; from rocks to bark to roots and shrubs. The more your little cage habitat resembles an Andes mountainside, the more homey and comfortable it will be to your small pet.

Cleaning the Cage

You should expect to spend at least fifteen to twenty minutes a day doing a basic clean: changing the water in the water sipper, washing the food and water containers with soapy water, and removing all droppings as well as wet or soiled sawdust or the soiled liner.

Take an hour or so out once a week to do a more thorough clean. Then, every six months, remove everything, sanitize it, and give the cage a complete bleaching with pet-safe cleaning agents. If your pet store does not have a good selection available, you can use a mixture of half vinegar to half water. Don't use standard supermarket cleaners, as these can be toxic to small animals.

Remember, anytime you get things wet, keep the chinchillas out of the cage till everything is nice and dry.

Chapter Three: Bringing Your Chinchilla Home

Covering Your Cage in the Day Time

Your daytime is the chinchilla's night, and without enough sleep it will become stressed and start exhibiting neurotic behavior. You can help block out the world by covering the cage with a light cotton cover in the daytime. Choose something that will allow air to circulate freely; the cage must not get warm.

Chapter Four: Caring for a Chinchilla

Your chinchilla home is lovingly prepared and standing ready. Now there is nothing left but to bring your new family member home and begin life together. But are you ready yourself for all that is involved?

How Chinchillas Behave in New Environments

For a prey animal like a chinchilla, moving into a new home is not going to be seen as fun and games and adventure. However friendly your little animal may be in the future, it is not going to start off its relationship with you by making the first moves, all pleased and excited and ready to get off on the right foot. A chinchilla in a new situation is mostly very, very scared.

Chapter Four: Caring For a Chinchilla

Your job in those first few weeks with your new chinchilla is to alleviate these fears, show it that there is nothing to be scared of, and show it you belong in a new category of friendly benevolence rather than the old category of 'bogeymen' with those owls, hawks and foxes.

Move carefully, and do not press things. Do not rush the relationship—the cage is enough of a new thing at first, and you need to give it time to explore it on its own terms.

There will be plenty of time later to let it out for exercise—after your chinchilla has adjusted to you and to a new home, you should do it daily. But do not start by taking it out the first day. Do not even try to hold it inside the cage. Rather, for the first week use a completely hands off approach—feed it, change its water, and talk to it gently through the walls of the cage, but do not get too close. Let it make its first impressions of you from your gentle voice as you watch from outside the cage.

Taming Your Chinchilla

Phase 1: The First Week

Taming your chinchilla begins in that first week, even as the little animal gets used to its new environment and you practice self-restraint and keep your hands off. You are not ignoring it; you are feeding it, giving it water, and keeping its home clean, but you are not grabbing it or even trying to touch it. All the time you work around the cage, you are talking in a low, reassuring, peaceful voice, letting it know

Chapter Four: Caring For a Chinchilla

you are there, that you care about it, and that you will give it space and its own time to come to you.

Phase 2: Good Connotations

Phase two begins when it has had a chance to adjust to its new home. This is when you get it used to you up-close and personal, while still refraining from any grabby chasing movements. You will also need to refrain, both now and later, from eye contact; to a prey animal like a chinchilla, this will be seen as a definite threat.

Prepare a treat for your little pet, and hold it carefully between the bars of the cage. Hold it there for some time, until it comes and gets it. You can speak to it; chinchillas can be trained to understand words. "Snack time, Chinii!" If it ignores it completely, put it away and try again another time. If it comes and smells it but is not quite brave enough to pick it out of your fingers, put it inside the cage for it to find and pick up later.

One important thing—a chinchilla is very prone to blood sugar swings and diabetes and cannot have many treats. One a day is the limit, and even then, not all of them can be sweets like raisins—one raisin a week is a good rule of thumb. There is a section on treats below; for now, just remember that, for the welfare of your pet, your generosity has to be held under tight rein.

Another point to note—after your chinchilla has been tamed you want to stop giving treats behind the bars of the cage; save them for more up-front and personal gifts. A

Chapter Four: Caring For a Chinchilla

chinchilla that is used to accepting treats in this way is liable to consider everything that comes in between the bars as food and will nip and bite any fingers that find their way in. This is not misbehavior; it is just a natural consequence of regular between-the-bars feeding.

Phase 3: Introducing Your Hand

Once your chinchilla is ready to take treats through the bars of the cage—and remember, it is likely to have taken a while, as it can only have one a day—it is time to get it accustomed to your hand. Again, you need baby steps.

First day, just open the cage door and put your hand in there. Just lay it there; do not move, not even your fingers. A chinchilla should come by to sniff or explore or even stand on it—and, being a curious little beast, it will, if you leave it there long enough.

Success depends more on your patience than anything else. Do not move, leave your arm limp, let it explore. When you cannot stand still any longer remove your arm gently. No goodbye petting is recommended.

Chapter Four: Caring For a Chinchilla

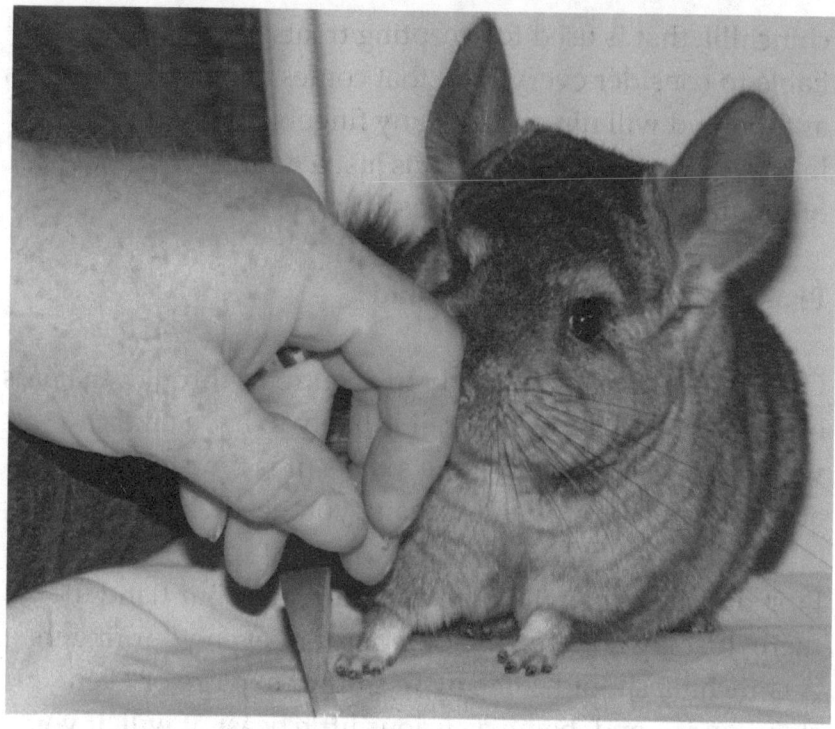

The second time you do it put the treat in the middle of your palm. Again leave your arm there as long as you comfortably can. If your chinchilla does not take the treat from your palm, just put it away and try it again later, or the next day. If it does, congratulations! You have achieved your first major milestone in chinchilla-taming; teaching your pet to eat out of your hand.

If it starts nipping at you, do not panic. This is not a hostile behavior; the chinchilla is accepting your hand as a new cage mate and attempting to groom you. It might take a bit of getting used to, but these friendly nips will not draw blood.

Chapter Four: Caring For a Chinchilla

Phase 4: First Scratches

This phase is when you first get to really touch your new pet, and it begins a day or two after your chinchilla has begun to eat out of your hand. Open the cage and put your hand in as before, and after the chinchilla comes up and takes the treat, and is exploring your hand, curl a finger up and gently scratch it around the ears or the side of the head. That is all. No grabbing, no major full-hand scratching, just a little one-finger scratch.

When you lift your finger and begin to scratch, be aware that it may get scared and run to the back of the cage again. If it does, let it! This is extremely important. It will come back again, and you have not lost anything. However, if you try to reach out and grab it, it will become terrified of you and you will lose all the gains you had made.

Where you go from here depends on its reaction. If it takes it well, keep on scratching, bringing even two or three fingers into play if you like. If it dashes away but comes right back, you can try again. If it dashes away and is away for a while, it is probably better to leave further scratching for tomorrow. Just leave your hand there for a few more minutes, still and limp, and then remove it gently and close the cage.

Soon your chinchilla will be comfortable with you petting and scratching, and will be comfortable eating from your palm and making exploratory journeys up your hand or arm. And then it is time for phase 5—letting your chinchilla out of the cage.

Chapter Four: Caring For a Chinchilla

Phase 5: Out and About

Before you begin this phase you will need to get ready in more than one way. You do not want to be scrambling for your guidebook when your chinchilla is running madly through the house, eating all of your electric cords or chewing the cover off the antique bible in the parlor. So before you let your chinchilla out, read this section on taming your chinchilla to the end.

Recommended reading will also include the section to follow, on holding your chinchilla, and also the follow-on section which covers what not to ever do. Additionally read the section several pages on, regarding exercising your chinchilla, making sure you read all the way through the part on getting it back in the cage.

Once that is read, you need to decide where to let your chinchilla out—and be sure it is a place that meets all the requirements for keeping both your chinchilla and your house safe. No electric cords anywhere. No access to anything that you do not want chewed, clawed, or urinated on.

For many new chinchilla owners, the best place may be the bathroom, without any electric devices or bottles-that-may-spill carefully stowed away, the lid down on the toilet, and both bathtub and sink empty and with the drains plugged up.

Chapter Four: Caring For a Chinchilla

Make sure you have plenty of time on your hands. Putting your chinchilla back in the cage is something that cannot be hurried, so plan accordingly. If you must leave the house for an important meeting in twenty minutes, this is not the time for your chinchilla's first outing.

When there is a block of time and you have chosen a place the chinchilla can be out in, you need to get the chinchilla there. For the first time, do not expect to carry it through the house to the bathroom and let it loose there, and then carry it back when it is finished. If its cage is at all moveable, take the whole thing into your chinchilla-proof space. Close the door, lock it, even, if there is a possibility unwitting family members may come by and let your pet out accidently. Then you can open the cage door, drape your hand inside, and let your chinchilla climb up your arm and into a free new world.

Note: If you are the sort who does not want to buy your chinchilla's affections with treats but would rather they came to you for your own merits, you can go through this same taming program without the tasty rewards. Skip feeding through the bars, and when you put your hand in there, just lay your empty hand down. The chinchilla's natural curiosity will come into play and it will come and explore and make friends with you whether or not you have a treat. Without a treat, it might take a little longer, but unless your animal was badly scarred by mistreatment before it came to you, you should meet with the same success.

Chapter Four: Caring For a Chinchilla

Holding a Chinchilla

The key to holding a chinchilla is to pick it up confidently, firmly, calmly, slowly, and gently. Chinchillas do not, as a rule, particularly like to be held; they are active little creatures and appreciate being in charge of their own mobility. But there are times when you will need to hold your chinchilla; and, after your chinchilla has become accustomed to its new house and has been tamed, it is useful to get some practice doing it.

There are two important things to remember not to do when you hold a chinchilla. First, never hold it by the tail. A chinchilla's tail is quite delicate and is meant to break off and free the chinchilla if a predator has it between its teeth. The same thing will happen if you try to grab the chinchilla by the tail. There will be blood, it will be ugly, and tails do not grow back.

Next, never pick it up by the scruff of the neck, like a kitten. This will initiate another defense mechanism, the fur slip, as it lets go of its fur in an instinctive effort to go free. It will come off on you, and you will be left with a very odd looking chinchilla. Fur does grow back, but it will take as long as six months.

It is better not to grab a chinchilla from above at all. Put your hand out, let your chinchilla begin exploring it, and then scoop it up with both hands from underneath and bring it up to your chest, with its back against your chest, and its front held gently by your hand. The rhythm of your breathing will help it to calm down. Be sure you are

Chapter Four: Caring For a Chinchilla

holding it firmly, because if it senses any uncertainty in your grasp it will try to jump out, and it has no idea of what is a safe distance to fall. Once it is comfortable though you should be able to hold it against your chest with one hand while using the other for whatever you need to do.

A less preferable way is to hold a chinchilla with one hand in the front, between the forepaws and hind legs, and the other hand over the back and holding firmly on the base of the tail.

This is a little less comfortable for the chinchilla and not safe for pregnant mothers, so if you have a female who may possibly be pregnant, do not hold it this way. A pregnant female should be carefully scooped up and carried close to your chest if it needs to be carried at all; but it is best to avoid as much handling as possible. Make sure you never put any pressure whatsoever on the abdomen of a pregnant mother.

How Not to Interact With Your Chinchilla

Your chinchilla may seem a feisty little fireball, but, inside, it is still a timid, delicate, scared little creature. It is important you never forget that this is a prey animal, an animal used, for untold centuries, to running from hunters. It is quite as aware that it is entirely in your power. Always treat your chinchilla gently. Any lapses, quick flashes of temper, or sudden shouts, spanks or scolding could have permanent damaging results.

Chapter Four: Caring For a Chinchilla

Suppose your chinchilla is doing something it should not and you shout at it, throw something at it or otherwise scare it. It does not have the mental wiring to connect the two events, and to understand that it was naughty and is now being punished. All it knows is that the enormous creature it had begun to mentally label as friendly benevolence, is in fact a big scary hunter. It will probably stop whatever the problematic behavior was and run and hide, but you will also have lost its trust.

If, on the other hand, you distract it in a nonthreatening way such as a clap or by calling to it with words it has come to understand, it will also (probably) stop the naughty behavior. And you will have retained its trust. If it does not obey you, you can also scoop it up gently from underneath, hold it to your chest, and remonstrate—gently—about how it is expected to behave. No, it is not likely to understand you, but it will be distracted and it will know it is loved.

Never scold your chinchilla, never hit or spank it, and never punish it by withholding food and water. Never chase it either. Chinchillas are extremely fast, and you are certain to scare it and lose whatever inroad you had been making on its affection. You are very unlikely to actually catch it that way.

Never, except in a dire emergency, catch it by throwing a blanket or sweater over it. This will bring it back to the Andes days when it fled from the hawk's black shadow, and those are memories you do not want associated with your presence.

Chapter Four: Caring For a Chinchilla

Another thing that is always counterproductive is trying to look your chinchilla in the eye. We people tend to consider looking in another's eye as a positive gesture; thousands of romance novels have eulogized about the power of just one lingering glance. But that is people culture, and it does not translate into chinchilla language. For a chinchilla, looking in the eye means just one thing: an ugly threat.

Bonding With Your Chinchilla

So now you have tamed your chinchilla and learned how to hold it: what is still needed for you two to really bond? Bonding is a very special process and there is no magic formula for it, but there are some essential ingredients.

Time – Spend time with your chinchilla; focused, quality time. Hang around the cage talking, let your arm dangle in the cage for hours, scarcely moving at first, then scratching around the chinchilla's head when it comes visiting. Be

Chapter Four: Caring For a Chinchilla

consistent about your time; spending a whole Saturday afternoon hovering around the chinchilla's cage and then ignoring it for the rest of the week will not work.

Gentleness— Be consistently gentle, and let all your movements be slow and measured. Introducing fear into the equation will completely hijack any attempts at bonding, so make sure your little animal feels safe always.

Speech—Talk to your chinchilla often in gentle, modulated tones. Use it name regularly. Talk while you clean the cage, while you change the water dish, and while you put fresh hay in the hayrack. Talk when you share the occasional treat.

Meet on its terms — Do not rush the bonding process. Giving it the opportunity to come to you and waiting for it to come will be much more effective than reaching out and grabbing. If you grab, it has only one thought—how to escape. If you wait, its curiosity takes over and it will come wandering over to explore.

Playing With Your Chinchilla

With all that in mind, then, what does playing with your chinchilla involve? Not exciting games of chase like you might do with your puppy. Not relaxing in the recliner together, as you might with your kitten or even your hamster. First of all, your chinchilla is too easily frightened and secondly, too excited and mobile.

Chapter Four: Caring For a Chinchilla

Playing with your chinchilla means letting it take the lead, and being willing to be a part of its fun and explorations. As you come to know your chinchilla and understand what it does and does not enjoy, playtime will become all the more fun.

Training Your Chinchilla

Training a chinchilla is not like training a cat or dog, but these small animals are very intelligent and can learn to understand and respond to short commands (no more than one or two syllables).

The first step in training your chinchilla is to teach it to answer to its name. Do not rush this; expect it to take several weeks. Just say its name once several times over, and when it responds—even if it is a small response—feed it a tiny piece of treat—half or a third of a daily allotment. Repeat this twice a day till it responds quickly whenever it hears its name.

You have seen chinchillas sit on their owner's shoulders, and you want yours to do it. This is not a behavior that needs to be trained into a chinchilla; it will do it on its own when it feels safe with you. The key is to give it lots of time. Sit quietly in the chinchilla's exercise room for at least an hour, and eventually it will come over and explore you. Avoid any sudden response or jerky movements as it climbs over you and perches on your shoulder as if it was a tree branch.

Chapter Four: Caring For a Chinchilla

Later, after it has got comfortable with climbing on your shoulder, you can teach it to do so on request by giving a one word command such as "Up!" and then setting the treat up there, in an obvious way, for it to find. Remember, it will take time for your chinchilla to understand your language, so be patient and do not get tired of repeating the same things over and over again.

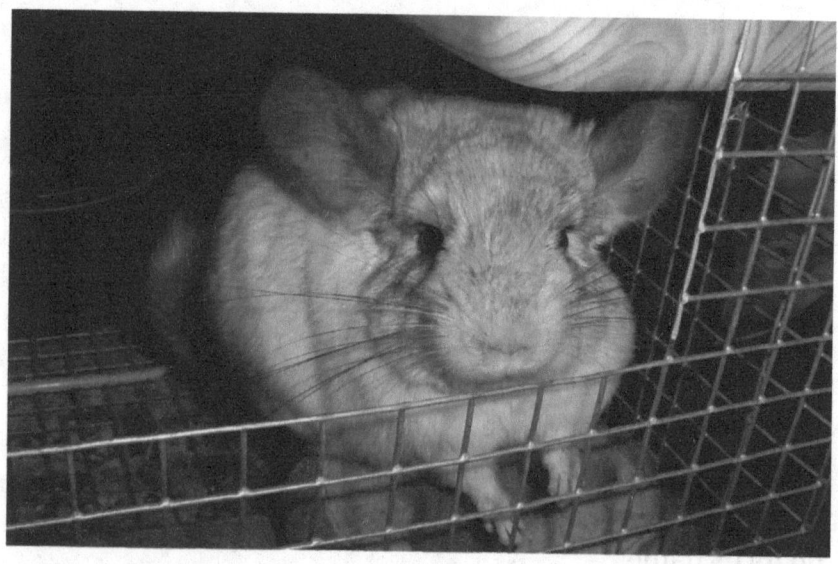

Toilet training—It is very difficult to train a chinchilla to use a litter box on your terms, but if you watch your chinchilla's own habits, you might be able to make a compromise system. Often a chinchilla will use one particular corner of the cage as bathroom. Once you know which corner that is, you can set a flat litter box there, and your chinchilla will probably continue using it and keep the rest of the cage (mostly) clean. It may help to put some soiled hay in the litter box to start with, so that the odor

Chapter Four: Caring For a Chinchilla

your chinchilla associates with its bathroom place is there already.

Feeding Your Chinchilla

Time for dinner! What does this mean for your new chinchilla friend? Not anything like what it means for you. Your chinchilla does not have mealtimes; it needs to be able to nibble throughout the day. And the food provided for it to eat has to be carefully chosen, because this exotic pet has a delicate stomach and very specific nutritional needs.

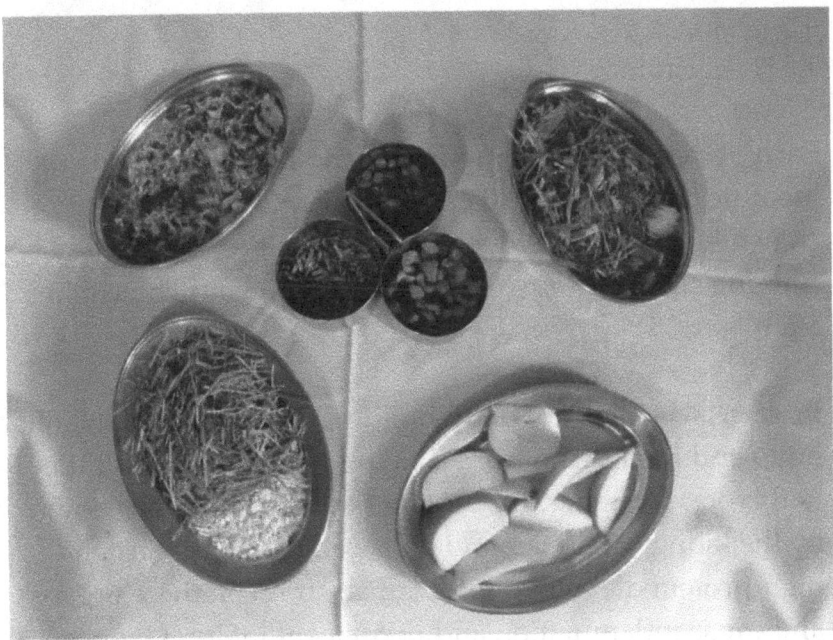

Try to provide fresh food at approximately the same time every day, for chinchillas thrive on routine. Throw out old food and wash the feed bowl to guard against bacterial growth.

Chapter Four: Caring For a Chinchilla

Nutritional Needs

The food your chinchilla gets must contain, every day, a very specific ratio of proteins, fiber, vitamins, and minerals.

Every day it must get:

15%	fiber	(15-35 %)
15%	protein	(<16%)
35%	carbohydrates	
4%	fat	
6%	minerals	
4%	sugar	
1.5%	calcium	

Each of these are very important, and too much of one or too little of the other will cause problems for your chinchilla. Fiber is needed to keep the digestive tract running smoothly as well as to file down your chinchilla's teeth.

Protein is needed as a body-builder, to help your chinchilla build and repair its muscles. No human diet for this little herbivore, though; extra protein needs to be broken down by the kidney and liver and disposed of, and a constant high-protein diet will put too much strain on these organs and cause inflammation and permanent internal damage.

Carbohydrates are the petrol that fuels their active life. Excess carbohydrate will be stored as fat and can cause obesity, but too little carbohydrates mean that your chinchilla will be slowly starving away.

Chapter Four: Caring For a Chinchilla

Minerals are necessary for all normal bodily functions, and calcium is necessary for a strong skeletal frame. Too much calcium, though, can be harmful for your chinchilla also, so everything in moderation.

Sugars should consist of no more than 4% of your chinchilla's daily intake. These little animals are very prone to diabetes, and feeding too much sugar will wreak havoc with their blood sugar levels. Remember that even hay contains some sugars.

How Much to Feed

Your chinchilla should get the nutrition it needs primarily from two sources: grass-based chinchilla pellets (1-2 tablespoons a day) and high quality fresh hay in unlimited quantities. They can be given additional fiber with unlimited branches of safe wood (see a discussion of safe and non-safe treats below).

Other treats have to be given in extremely limited quantity. A small raisin or cranberry once a week and a raisin size piece of apple, carrot or other root vegetable on other days is as much as your chinchilla's little body can take. It may be better to give treats only once every other day.

Chapter Four: Caring For a Chinchilla

Types of Food

Hay

Hay will always be your chinchilla's staple food, for it comes closest to providing the perfect mix of nutrients for your little pet. Most of the time, you will probably be feeding your chinchilla timothy hay, a hay made of dried grasses. This hay is high fiber, and the proportion of vitamins and minerals it contains make it a very near ideal food for your little pet.

There are times when a chinchilla needs a richer diet—during the first six months of growth for a weanling, during pregnancy and while lactating, or sometimes at the end of a long life. For those times alfalfa hay is better.

Alfalfa hay is not your standard hay; it looks more like dried weeds. It is lower in fiber and higher in energy and protein than timothy hay, and also higher in some trace minerals and in calcium.

Make sure the hay you give your chinchilla is fresh, crisp, and green-colored, not limp and yellow. Moldy or stale hay can cause life-threatening problems such as stomach ulcers.

Pellets

Pellets are to hay what the slice of cheese is to your sandwich bread—a little extra highly concentrated goodness, just to make sure your chinchilla is getting what it needs. Buy chinchilla pellets rather than those sold for

Chapter Four: Caring For a Chinchilla

rabbits or guinea pigs; the nutritional needs of these animals are different.

If you have options, give your chinchilla timothy-hay based pellets when feeding its alfalfa hay, and alfalfa-based pellets when feeding timothy hay based pellets. Rather than keep your pellets in the open bag they came in, move them to a re-sealable plastic bag and keep the bag closed between feeds to make sure it does not go stale.

Mixed feeds

These are combination feed mixes, often sold in pet stores. People like them because it makes them feel as if they were giving their pets options and variety. They are no good for chinchillas, because these little creatures have no idea what is good for them.

Imagine serving your two-year-old toddler a choice of either a chocolate fudge cake or a vegetable dish. Is there much chance the little guy will go for the vegetables? Your chinchilla has about the same capability of making a sensible choice as a toddler does. If given a choice, it will pick out all the tasty bits and end up with big nutritional imbalances. Stick with the boring looking pellets, and save treats for special occasions.

Chinchillas need a fairly stable diet, and sudden change can cause stomach upsets. If you need to change the brand of food that you give to your chinchilla, then make the change gradually. Start by giving 25% of the new brand and 75% of the old, then go to 50%-50%, the next day to 75%-25%, and by the fourth or fifth day you will have switched over entirely.

Caecotrophs

Your chinchilla needs to digest its food twice in order to get the nutrition it needs from it, and it does this by eating its droppings. You will notice it produces two types: caecotrophs, or wet droppings, and drier 'twice-baked' droppings that no longer have anything it needs in them.

This part of the chinchilla's diet is not your responsibility; it will generate its own caecotrophs and eat them. Just be aware that this is perfectly normal and necessary to its digestion.

Treats

There is nothing wrong with treats—in moderation. The problem with treats and chinchillas, though, is that what seems to you a very small taste of something, to your little animal's metabolic system, can be an enormous overload. Take one tiny little raisin. The sugar this contains is the equivalent, in human terms, of one big cupful of table sugar.

Chapter Four: Caring For a Chinchilla

Your chinchilla shouldn't have more than one raisin a week. Yes, that is right, limit it to one a week. You can choose one sweet day—Sunday, perhaps, if that is a special day in your house—and on that day let it have either a small raisin or a dried cranberry. Other days you may give your chinchilla treats that are lower in sugar—a raisin-sized piece of carrot one day, a goji berry another day, and a third day, a rosehip for an extra dose of vitamin C.

If you feel overly constrained by this, and as if you absolutely must give more treats, you can hand-feed your chinchilla with the pellets that you have chosen to supplement its diets with. But it should get those pellets anyway, so after you have finished doling out, one by one, however many you have patience for, make sure you pour the remainder into its feed bowl for it to eat in its own time.

Safe in any quantity: hay, pieces of safe wood such as apple or mulberry.

Chapter Four: Caring For a Chinchilla

Safe in appropriate quantity: chinchilla pellets.

Safe in careful moderation: *(one raisin size piece per day of any of:)* bits of apple, carrot, or turnip, goji berries, rosehips, dried marshmallow root, dried dandelion leaves or root, dried rosemary, raw oatmeal or barley.

Dangerous in any amounts: sweet breakfast cereal, chocolate, candy, nuts, green vegetables such as spinach, tree bark, corn, wood of unsafe trees, pinecones.

Wood is a wonderful treat for your chinchilla, because those ever-growing teeth need filing down. There are safe and unsafe woods, so make sure you know where the branch came from. See the lists under the Dental Care section.

Exercising Your Chinchilla

Your chinchilla needs lots and lots of exercise. It is not just for good looks or to avoid obesity; exercise is important for mental health too. If your chinchilla does not get the exercise it needs, it will become neurotic, start acting strange, and is liable to get into damaging habits such as fur biting.

You can help your chinchilla exercise in its cage by making it as roomy as possible, with a number of different shelves and levels, and also by providing an exercise wheel.

Chapter Four: Caring For a Chinchilla

Exercise Wheels

Do you ever get that feeling in your legs when you feel you just must run, far and fast? Believe me, if you were stuck in a little four by six room day after day, you would get that feeling regularly. And so does your chinchilla. Providing an exercise wheel means you are enabling it to run when the urge hits, and it is one of the best ways to fight boredom and listless behaviors.

Your chinchilla needs a fairly big exercise wheel, so fitting it into the cage may be a bit of a headache. However, if there is any way you can manage it, it is definitely worth doing. There are a number of safety rules you should keep in mind as you go wheel-shopping.

The exercise wheel should be metal, and at least 14 inches in diameter—preferably larger. The running surface should be at least 5 inches wide. Do not let your chinchilla run on a wheel made of wire mesh; its toes will get caught between the wires, causing damage. Any wheels used for a chinchilla should be completely solid.

Your wheel should not have a central axel, as this can trap the chinchilla's tail. The wheel must be well secured; and placed so there is no danger of your chinchilla getting stuck underneath. Putting a shelf above it is a good idea; otherwise, a chinchilla landing on the top while the wheel is in motion could get badly hurt.

Another option is to buy your chinchilla a flying saucer. These look like a pan lid mounted on a spinner, and are usually made entirely of metal. Using a flying saucer is much easier on your chinchilla's back than using an exercise wheel, and for adult chinchillas, safer. However, the flat design means that it will take up more space than a regular exercise wheel would, and it is harder for a chinchilla to learn how to use. Some never get the hang of it.

Mount your flying saucer near the floor of your cage for a safe setup.

The flying saucer is dangerous for small kits, so remove it anytime you expect newborns.

Letting Your Chinchilla Out of the Cage

Making the cage conducive to exercise is important for your chinchilla, but, unless you have the resources to change one of your bedrooms into a full-size chinchilla cage, it is not enough. This mountain rodent needs to be able to exercise all its muscles every now and then—even those it uses for six foot jumps!

Ideally, you should let your chinchilla out of the cage every day for at least an hour, preferably two. It will need to be supervised at all times, but that does not mean you have to spend the whole time watching—it is perfectly fine to let it play while you read a book or do some home-based chores. You need to be there, though, and the room must be chinchilla-safe.

Chapter Four: Caring For a Chinchilla

What does chinchilla-safe mean? Firstly, it must be contained; no doors, windows, or vents through which it might slip out into the big scary outdoors. Secondly, there can be no danger.

One big issue is electric cords; if your chinchilla finds them, it will eat them, and the voltage that goes through a little body will be an extremely high amount.

Once you have checked that there is nowhere your little chinchilla could hurt itself, make sure there is nothing it could hurt. Be aware that it will be jumping, climbing, and running all over the room, sampling everything, chewing on what seems tasty, and leaving urine or droppings wherever the urge hits it. Put away anything irreplaceable, and cover immoveable items with chinchilla-safe covers.

If your walls are wallpaper, paint, or another easily destructible substance you may want to line them, up to a foot and a half or two feet high, with cardboard boxes. If

Chapter Four: Caring For a Chinchilla

the floor is carpeted and you do not want urine stains, cover your floor.

When you bring it out of its cage your chinchilla will run about exploring everything, and then is likely to settle down for more in-depth examinations of special things that capture its interest.

To avoid mischief, make sure there is plenty for it to do. Take toys out of the cage and scatter them over the floor. Add some rocks you pick up on a neighborhood walk, and some chinchilla-safe branches. Carpet rolls, available at places where they sell bulk carpet, are great fun for a chinchilla to go in and out of.

Returning Your Chinchilla to the Cage

It has had its run, and now it is time for it to go back—but how to catch it? This may well be the trickiest part of exercising your chinchilla: returning it to the cage when the exercise is done. You should not chase it. It is faster than you, anyway, and a romp around the room will only scare it.

The best and easiest way, is to wait for it to be ready, and then invite it back to the cage. Put away the cage toys and chew sticks you scattered around the room at the beginning of the session so it can have a hint that playtime is over.

Chapter Four: Caring For a Chinchilla

You can plan feeding time so that it coincides with the end of the exercise session, and if you do this regularly, it will decide when to end the time out itself and go back to the cage to wait for supper. If you have not gone through your daily allotted treat (remember, no more than one a day!) before exercise time is over, you can use it then also, and call your chinchilla to you at the cage to enjoy a little morsel.

Another technique is to do your dust bathing just after exercise time. Set the container you use for dust baths out where your chinchilla can see it, and shake it a little after putting the dust in. Chinchillas absolutely love baths, and it will probably make a beeline for it. After it is enjoying a bath, gently pick up the entire container and move it into the cage, then close the door. Remove the dust bath after the bath is over.

Chapter Four: Caring For a Chinchilla

If you are having a lot of trouble putting your chinchilla back, it may be that it is not getting enough exercise. Try to plan for longer out times. If you are having a hard time being patient while the chinchilla runs around, work on making supervising your chinchilla more comfortable for yourself. If the bathroom is the room you decided on as your chinchilla safe place, for example, you can put an air mattress in the bathtub and borrow a good novel from the library to read just during exercise sessions.

Shedding

Chinchillas shed year round, and this heightens in the warm summer months. The new coat often begins to grow in around the head and then works its way down, and sometimes you can see a distinct line between the old and new coats. They get a new coat approximately every three months, so do not be surprised by a moderate amount of shedding.

If there is more shedding than usual or your chinchilla starts looking very patchy you are likely to be having a problem. Chinchillas lose their fur if they are worried or stressed and they chew their fur off if they are bored, so it could be a mental issue. There is also the possibility of a skin fungus such as ringworm (see the chapter on chinchilla health, below).

Chapter Four: Caring For a Chinchilla

Dust Baths

A chinchilla should be given a dust bath about every other day, and at least twice a week. A chinchilla is a very clean animal, and a dust bath is part of their natural grooming routine. Up in the Andes Mountains, they would roll about in volcanic dust. Here in your living room, you can make a pretty good substitute with a large vase or fish bowl of dust.

Your dust bath should be a sturdy, non-tippable container with a side opening large enough for a chinchilla to get in (think, a fishbowl tipped on its side). There needs to be enough room inside for the chinchilla to roll around and enjoy itself, but not so much that the dust gets scattered. Most pet stores sell little plastic dust bath houses, and these work fine, as you are not leaving them inside the cage for the chinchilla to chew on.

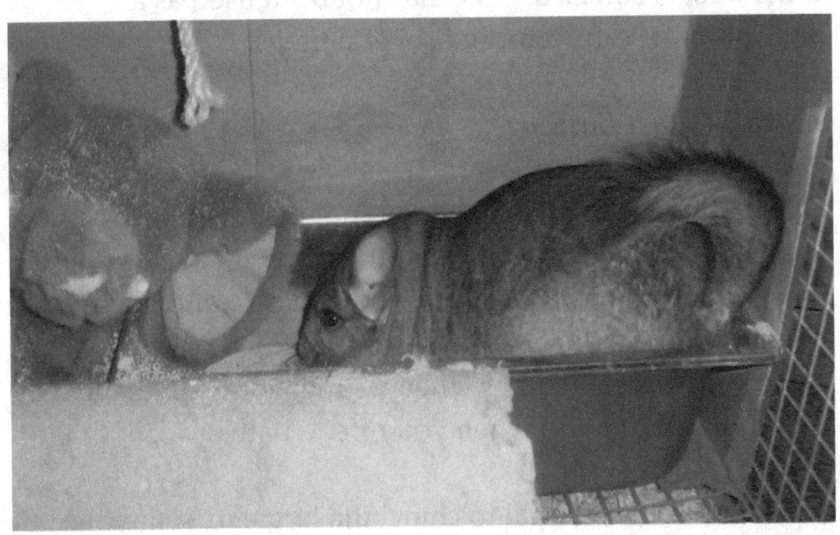

Chapter Four: Caring For a Chinchilla

Buy chinchilla dust at your pet store. You can substitute with sand or kitchen materials in a pinch, but those substitutes will only clean the surface of your chinchilla's fur and not get down between the individual hairs. They may also irritate the eyes.

Commercially-sold chinchilla dust is made to replicate the volcanic dust in the Andes Mountains, and it is fine enough to permeate all the way down to the chinchilla's skin, cleaning as it goes.

To give your chinchilla a bath, all you do is fill your bath house with about an inch of the fine chinchilla dust and put the whole bath into the cage. The chinchilla will climb in itself and start rolling, after which it will groom itself. Ten or fifteen minutes later, after the chinchilla comes out, you remove the dust bath and put it away until next time.

If the dust is still clean—i.e. has not been used as a bathroom—it can be reused several times.

Teaching Dust Bathing

Dust bathing is learned behavior, not instinctual; your chinchilla learned it from its mother. If you have a chinchilla who has not been well taken care of, who lived in a home where a dust bath was not provided or who was removed from its mother when young, your chinchilla may not know what to do when you offer a bath.

Dust baths are essential to chinchilla hygiene, so if your chinchilla does not know what to make of it, it is up to you

Chapter Four: Caring For a Chinchilla

to take mommy's place and teach it. Do not force it in the bath though. Rather, if it shows hesitancy about going in, simply take some of the dust and put it in a soup bowl or other open container, and set this in the cage for a few days.

Your chinchilla will leap in at some point out of curiosity, and when it rolls around to get back up will discover what fun it is. After a bit of exploration there it will be ready to go in the dust bath, and you can take the bowl back out of the cage.

Dental Care

If your full-grown chinchilla is getting enough calcium, its teeth will be carrot orange. A white color means calcium deficiency, and you will need to rethink the diet and possibly give supplements. The teeth of healthy young chinchillas may be white.

The key to dental care for your chinchilla is simply providing plenty of things to gnaw on. A chinchilla's teeth, growing at a rate of 3 inches a year, need to be kept within a certain length if they are to fit in its mouth. The teeth also need to be worn down, so they are not unduly sharp. Timothy hay contains wonderfully rough, fibrous grass stalks to chew on and should be part of every chinchilla's diet, but even that is not enough. You should provide your little teether with a continuous supply of pumice stones and twigs, branches and wooden toys.

What it chews, it eats, so anything you give your chinchilla for a chew toy should be edible. No paints, glosses, or

Chapter Four: Caring For a Chinchilla

polishes. Make sure any wood comes from safe trees; some wood contains essential oils that can be dangerous to your pet.

Safe woods: apple, pear, mulberry, cottonwood, elm, dogwood, hazelnut, kiwi, kiln-dried pine, bamboo, willow.

Unsafe woods: cedar, cherry, peach, plum, chestnut, walnut, yew, teak, sycamore, sandalwood, rosewood, fresh pine, oak, maple, fir, juniper, eucalyptus, citrus woods, elderberry, birch, cashew, beech, almond.

Chapter Five: Breeding Chinchillas

Basic Breeding Information

Breeding chinchillas can be an enormously rewarding enterprise, but it is not simple, straightforward, or easy, and you need to know what you are getting into and be sure you are ready for it before you begin.

First, do you have the space for it? It would be easy if you could put your growing family of chinchillas in one big cage—they fit there, physically—but in actual practice chinchillas are not good at sharing space. Even if you are just breeding one pair of chinchillas to get one set of kits, you need to have separate cages to give mother and father their own space when they need it, and you need to be prepared to separate brother and sister kits as well. Since each of these separate groupings needs a cage big enough

Chapter Five: Breeding Chinchillas

to run, play, and exercise, you are talking about a lot of room.

Next, do you have the time for it? If all goes well and nature follows her own sweet course, you may have little more to do other than take care of the additional chinchillas and spend a few minutes here and there moving chinchillas around and keeping things safe. But if you decide to go into breeding, you have to be prepared for the times when things do not go so well.

You will need to take out the time to take your chinchilla mother to the hospital should there be a problem. You need to be ready to foot the bill if it needs expensive treatment. And if it does not make it or is unable to take care of all her kits, you need to be able to play surrogate mother to the little ones.

What surrogate mother means, among other things, is medicine-dropper feedings every two hours round the clock until the kits get on their feet. Are you ready to take on that kind of responsibility?

Even if you have the space, time, and emergency-money, there is still one issue left. What will happen to the kits when they grow up? If you are planning to sell them, do you have buyers? If you are planning to give them away, do you have responsible, knowledgeable people who will be ready to commit to their care? Remember, a chinchilla can live between ten or twenty years, so each little one born to you will be a big responsibility.

Chapter Five: Breeding Chinchillas

If, in spite of all it entails, you feel certain you want to go on with this project, there are some things you need to know. The first thing we will look at here is chinchilla genetics, as there are things that you should be aware of before you begin pairing up males and females. After we have looked at that, we will go on to the nitty-gritty of putting mom and dad together and letting the breeding process begin.

Genetics

You may have failed your genetics course in college, but you should still be able to get a handle on what is happening in the DNA of the chinchillas that are going to be born to you. You need to, if you are going to breed chinchillas responsibly. We'll start off here with a few simple definitions.

Genotype: the specific genetic makeup of an individual; the codes that give directions for genetically based physical traits, including fur color, eye color, and type of fur.

Phenotype: the way a genotype is expressed in an individual; the physical characteristics of the individual.

Locus: the place on the chromosome that contains alleles (genes) coding for various physical characteristics. For example, the locus that holds the alleles for fur color, or for eye color, or for body type. Each locus contains two alleles, which determine the physical trait that will be expressed in the individual.

Chapter Five: Breeding Chinchillas

Alleles: also known as genes, these are the actual coding or 'directions,' present in the chromosome that determines specific physical traits. While each locus contains two alleles, only one may be expressed. Or they may both exert partial influence for a mixed phenotype.

Dominant: an allele is dominant if it is always the one expressed when paired at a locus with a recessive allele.

Recessive: an allele is recessive if it is not expressed when paired on a locus with a dominant allele.

Heterozygous: a genotype is heterozygous for a particular trait if the locus contains two different alleles.

Homozygous: a genotype is homozygous for a particular trait if the locus contains two identical alleles.

Now that we have all that down, let us look at how it relates to chinchillas. Unlike breeders of dogs, horses, or cows, chinchilla breeders have historically focused on a single locus: the one which determines fur color.

To make it even simpler, there is just one standard for fur color: the original grey color that these little rodents had in the Andes Mountains. All other colors are mutations. There are nine or ten basic mutations recognized by breeders, and pretty much all the shades and colors that chinchillas are today are simply combinations of these.

The codes for the various mutations are as follows:

Chapter Five: Breeding Chinchillas

Black (or TOV)	Bl
White	W
Beige	Pw
Ebony	B
Charcoal	b
Violet	v
Sapphire	s
Pink-eyed Beige	p
Black-eyed Beige	pr

Mutations coded with capital letters are dominant; those coded with small letters are recessive. Ebony is what is called weakly dominant.

Standard contains a 'perfect gene' with none of these mutations, so the genotype of a standard is written as blbl/ww/pwpw/bb/BB/VV/SS/PP/PrPr. Notice that in each slot you have the capitalization opposite of each mutational code. Since a white mutation is coded by W, the absence of a white mutation is coded by w. Since the presence of a violet mutation is coded by v, the absence of it is coded by V. Therefore the absence of any mutation is the opposite of all mutations, and denoted as the opposite of each mutation code.

Writing down the genotype of any mutation chinchilla could be a similarly long process. We could code a hetero black chinchilla as Blbl/ww/pwpw/bb/BB/VV/SS/PP/PrPr. But for brevity's sake, convention has it that for mutants we only write down the specific part of the code that is relevant to the mutations. For our hetero black we ignore the part of the genotype that is equivalent to standard, and write Blbl to express that one of the standard alleles is carrying the Black dominant mutation.

Imagine, for simplicity's sake, that your chinchilla has a secret pocket containing two cards, representing the two pertinent alleles at the locus we are focusing on. These cards are either blank (think standard) or have letters on them; the case specific name of a particular mutation.

The cards contained in your chinchilla's secret pocket determine what it looks like. If the name on one card is capitalized (dominant) and the other is lowercase (recessive), the capitalized one is the one expressed and the lower case card just has to sit there. If both contain capital letters or both are lowercase, they share the responsibility of determining the color and appearance of your chinchilla.

Your blank standard cards have less priority than the cards with the capitalized letters and more priority than the lowercase cards, so a chinchilla will only look standard if one of his cards is blank and the other is either blank or lowercase.

When mom and dad chinchilla have babies, they will copy one of their two cards and pass it on to baby. So baby gets one card from dad, one from mom. These cards could be either capitalized, with lower case letters, or blanks. A dominant allele is not any more likely to be passed on than a recessive allele. But when the baby gets his two cards, if one contains capital letters and the other contains small letters, it is the one with capital letters that gets to express itself in baby's phenotype, or physical appearance.

Chapter Five: Breeding Chinchillas

Do you get the picture? We use Punnett squares to give us a visual for what we can expect to happen when mom and dad get together and copy their cards for the little guys. Here we have a violet dad with two recessive violet alleles (vv), and a standard mom with one violet mutation gene (Vv). Since the violet gene is recessive, she does not look violet, but some of her children do:

	V	v
V	Vv	Vv
v	vv	vv

Half of the children are violet like dad, and the other half will be standard chinchillas that carry the recessive violet allele.

The Lethal Factor

The two-card system is designed so if there are mis-copies and therefore mistakes in the genetic information expressed in one allele, the other allele at that locus can cover for that. If there are two identical alleles, however, you have the mis-type twice over, and a high potential for trouble.

This is the case with white and TOV alleles. A chinchilla with one white or one TOV allele paired with a standard allele, can be perfectly healthy. The white and TOV alleles are dominant, so they are fully expressed in the phenotype in spite of being on only one card. If you pair two white chinchillas, though, you have a 25% of having a baby with two white alleles.

Chapter Five: Breeding Chinchillas

Two white alleles—or two TOV alleles—is not compatible with life. There will be a spontaneous abortion and the baby will probably be reabsorbed by the mother at an early stage. If it is reabsorbed incompletely, it can rot inside the mother, give her a bacterial infection, and cause her to go into toxic shock and die.

Either way, it will never be born alive.

Pairings between two whites or two TOVs should be avoided. If you pair a white and a standard, half the offspring (statistically speaking) will still be white, because white is a dominant mutation.

The Breeding Process

Before you begin breeding, be sure your chinchillas are compatible and that they are ready to become parents. Your female chinchilla, especially, must be completely healthy if she is going to take on the big job of starting a new life. She needs to be old enough, too, and that is more than being sexually mature. A chinchilla will have ovulation cycles and go into heat from the time she is around twelve weeks old, but will not be fully ready to be a mother until she is at least eight months.

A female chinchilla usually knows when she is ready to begin bearing children, and before that time comes, she will fight off any males who try to mate with her. So if she is acting feisty, let her be alone. Mating is a thing that should not be rushed.

Chapter Five: Breeding Chinchillas

Before you pair her up you should check her pelvis size to make sure any kits will be able to be born. To do this, hold her by the base of the tail. The little round depression below the tail is the pelvic bone. It should be no smaller than the size of a dime; the size of a (relatively small) thumb; place your thumb over it to check its size.

The male you are hoping to pair with her should be smaller than her, not bigger. Females grow faster than males, so this means her mate should be the same age or younger. A bigger male can force your female into mating when she is not ready, with disastrous consequences both for their offspring and for your female's future mating capabilities.

Buying a young pair from the pet shop tends to be problematic because kits you find at the same store may well be brothers and sisters, and the pet store owner may not even be aware of their parentage.

Buying from a reliable breeder who is willing to give you detailed information about the parentage and history of both your male and female is highly recommended if you intend to do breeding yourself.

Mating chinchillas

Even after you have determined your male and female are healthy, genetically compatible, not at risk of inbreeding and of the right age, mating chinchillas is not quite as simple as putting the two of them in the same cage and shutting the door. To begin with, you need to first ensure

Chapter Five: Breeding Chinchillas

that your prospective mom and dad can live with each other without killing one another.

Start with the two of them in separate cages, and put the two cages next to each other but not touching. Leave an inch or so between, so there is no danger whatsoever of violent contact. Then keep them there for a week or two, giving them a chance to get used to the other's presence.

If you have had a week or so with no hostilities, move the cages together so that they are touching. Again, leave them alone for a while. Once they have lived peacefully side by side for another week, it is time to bring them together for real. Because chinchillas are extremely territorial, it is best if their first meeting can be in a place that neither of them own. If you have another spare cage that would be a wonderful option; if not, let them have their outside exercise together so that they can meet on neutral ground.

If this first meeting goes well you can work on deodorizing whichever cage you want them in together, and re-introducing them there. Deodorizing is important because chinchillas rely primarily on scent to tell ownership. If you have taken away that away, or mixed up the smell of both of them, they will be able to view the cage as something that is jointly owned.

Even after they seem to be living peacefully together you will still need to monitor your new pair. When your female goes into heat, your male will be desperate to mate with her, and she may decide not to let him. If she is bigger, and she should be, she will be able to take charge of the

Chapter Five: Breeding Chinchillas

situation, and you should remain in the background, letting them sort themselves out. You may have to wait some time, but when she is ready to become a mother, she will mate.

Mating is usually a fairly intense, aggressive process, but if the two of them are getting violent enough that blood is drawn it is time to remove your male for a while.

If they do mate, there will be a waxen plug inserted in the female's vaginal canal to keep in the semen, and this falls out within a few days. If you find it while cleaning up the cage you will know that they have been together, though you will not know yet if your female is pregnant. It should be a narrow, cream colored object about an inch long.

After mating you need to check your male for a hair ring around his penis. Because a large amount of fur is lost during mating, and some of this sometimes forms into a ring around the penis, and as he tries to remove it, it usually only becomes tighter. This can lead to intense pain and even death if ignored. If there is a ring, lubricate with a little Vaseline and then carefully tease it open and, when you can get the blade of fine scissors in there, cut it open and off. If you cannot manage it yourself you will need to pay a visit to the vet.

Pregnancy Period

A mother chinchilla carries her babies for around 111 days. What this means is that if you find a wax plug, you will know that, if your chinchillas were successful at baby-making, you can expect kits in a little less than four months.

Chapter Five: Breeding Chinchillas

It will be some time before you have confirmation either way. Both chinchillas will carry on as before, and it takes some time for mother to begin to gain weight.

There are many times you might not find the wax plug; if you use wood shavings for flooring, for instance, it can easily be thrown away with the garbage.

The first period of fetal growth is slow, and you will not be able to tell much from the outside. Thirty days in, the chinchilla fetus weighs only 0.1 gram (0.003 ounces). At 45 days, ten days later, it will have grown a ten-fold factor and be 1 gram (0.03 ounces), but still tiny. Sixty days sees him at 10 grams (0.3 ounces).

Around twelve weeks into pregnancy the mother chinchilla will begin to act differently. She will suddenly become excited about food and start eating significantly more. Her nipples will begin to redden and lengthen, until by the time of birth they are as long as her fur. The baby inside her will start growing quickly, and this will become evident in the size of her abdomen. Toward the end of pregnancy you may even see the kits move inside of her.

Care of the mother chinchilla primarily involves keeping her stress levels down and making sure she gets all the nutrition she needs. Handle her as little as possible, and never palpate her abdomen, as this could trigger miscarriage. If you need to pick her up make sure to scoop her up very gently.

Chapter Five: Breeding Chinchillas

Buying a digital scale and weighing her every other day is a good way of monitoring her health during pregnancy. You will want a scale with a sturdy base, on which you can place a Tupperware or similar container to hold your chinchilla securely while she is being weighed. Always weigh at approximately the same time of day.

Make sure she gets the food she needs, and that it is of the highest quality. Substituting alfalfa for the regular timothy hay is often a good idea doing high-growth periods like pregnancy. Giving a calcium and vitamin C supplement is also recommended.

Preparing for Birthing

There are two important things to prepare with an impending chinchilla birth. First, let the mother prepare her body for the big event. During the last part of her pregnancy she will suddenly become very hungry, and it is important that she has continual access to healthy, high-quality, appropriate food.

You should also prepare the cage. Although a chinchilla's cage must always be kept cool and breezy, when you are expecting a birth you must also be careful the cage does not get too cold and there are no drafts. Kits, like newborn humans, are born wet. Their wet fur takes its time to dry, and for a newborn kit unaccustomed to regulating its own temperature, cold can kill.

The cage side mesh should be no bigger than ½ inch by 1 inch, and the floor should be completely solid.

Chapter Five: Breeding Chinchillas

Make sure the cage is baby-proof; take away from the cage anything that could be a hazard to newborn kits. If you use a water dish rather than a sipper, decrease the amount of water in it and fill it more frequently to make sure your chinchillas stay hydrated. A newborn chinchilla could tumble into a full water dish and drown. If you use a flying saucer for exercise, remove it till the kits are grown and have had some time to grow.

If you usually leave your dust bath in the cage, take it out now. The mother chinchilla should not have a bath for a week before, and a week after the kits are born, or the dust may cause infections or interfere with the kits nursing.

You may want to take out your shelves, so that mother does not go upstairs and leave the little ones out in the cold. If you leave them in, be sure to monitor the situation carefully.

Chapter Five: Breeding Chinchillas

As birth nears, the mother will probably become very unsociable, and may be even become aggressive. She may stay inside the nest box, coming out only to eat or drink. These can be signs that the kits are only a day or two from being born, and you should give her the space she needs.

Birth

Birth usually happens early in the morning. The mother chinchilla will get very agitated as her labor pains increase; during this time it is best to leave her completely alone and observe her quietly. There may be only five or ten minutes of intense labor before birth, or it may take a few hours; the average is probably half an hour. When they are ready to be born she will pull out her kits, cut their umbilical cords with her teeth, and, if they were born in a sac, remove that.

The birth of additional kits can follow in quick succession, with five minutes or even less between births, or there can be an interval of an hour.

The kits should be completely formed, with all their fur and even with teeth. The size they are born depends on many factors, nutritional and genetic; they can weigh from twenty to a hundred grams (0.70 to 3.5 ounces) at birth. The average birth weight is about 35 grams (1.2 ounces).

Chinchillas usually have small litters, and single births are completely normal. There may be up to six kits, but usually there will be one or two.

Chapter Five: Breeding Chinchillas

After each kit is born, a placenta (afterbirth) will come out. This will probably look like a shapeless bloody mass, and the mother will probably eat it to help restore her body after the birth. This is perfectly natural and even necessary to her health, so do not take it from her.

She will be focused on her kits, drying them, warming them, and feeding them. If the kits are having trouble getting warm and dry you can help; your presence will not make the mother reject them. Under most circumstances, though, she will do a fine job herself. She will also clean herself up, and then rest. Make sure she has a peaceful environment.

Possible Birthing Complications

While usually everything will go smoothly during a chinchilla birth, you must be watchful and prepared in case something goes wrong.

Sometimes the waters may break before the mother goes into labor. Your mother chinchilla will be picking at her birth opening, attempting, without any success, to extract the babies; her nose will be wet. If labor does not start on its own immediately, you will need to call the vet.

A flow of blood from the birth opening before the babies are born is also a sign of trouble, and the mother will need medical attention.

Sometimes a kit will be stillborn or partly mummified. In this case, simply remove the dead kit immediately.

Chapter Five: Breeding Chinchillas

Sometimes part of the placenta or a dead fetus is retained. The dead tissue will rot inside the mother, causing a bacterial infection. The mother chinchilla will probably have a high fever, swollen genitals, and a foul-smelling vaginal discharge of mucus and pus. She may lose her appetite, not be able to provide milk to her kits, and have difficulty walking. In such a case the mother must be brought to the vet immediately. She will receive medicine to help her eject the infected tissue, and antibiotics to deal with the infection.

Sometimes a kit is born very much weaker and smaller than the others, and from the beginning does not seem to have much zest in life. Such a kit may die overnight, or within the first three days. There is usually nothing that can be done; such kits are usually genetically weak and unable to survive.

If a baby is born in a birth sac the mother will almost always bite it off and clean and dry the baby. The exception might be a very young mother who does not have fully functional maternal instincts yet, or who is what we might term mentally undeveloped. If you notice a situation like this, free the baby from the sac yourself and dry and warm him. Inside the sac it cannot breathe and will soon die of suffocation if left on its own.

Postnatal Care

When the babies are born the chief concern is warmth: a baby that is too cold will die. Do not overdo this and put

Chapter Five: Breeding Chinchillas

the electric heater on next to the chinchilla cage. Chinchillas can die from overheating.

Make sure the mother is well-fed. Do not give her a dust bath for a week, but make sure she is comfortable in every way. Let her have peace and quiet, and a bit of time alone to get to know her babies.

Chinchilla kits will start nursing immediately after being born, but it may take some time for the mother's milk to come in. This is normal, and the kits are born with enough reserves to enable them to survive up to three days without milk. Since a mother chinchilla has six teats it is possible for all her kits to nurse at once. Sometimes, though, one gets left out and cannot seem to get its share of milk. If this seems to be the case, you can supplement with cat or goat milk, available in powder form from your pet store.

As the kits are born with all their teeth and are not the most gentle nurslings, the mother's nipples should be checked for bites or infections. Minor cuts can be dealt with at home with antibiotic cream and warm compresses. If, though, the nipple is enlarged, stiff, warm to the touch and apparently painful, it is mastitis — a milk duct infection. In such case mother will need to be given antibiotics, and if she cannot nurse her kits you will need to hand feed them.

If, a few hours after the birth, a baby seems ignored and his eyes are still glued shut, or it is unwashed you should take him out, rub him down gently with soft toweling, and wipe his eyes carefully with a damp washcloth. Return him to his mother after you have got him clean.

Chapter Five: Breeding Chinchillas

A mother chinchilla will usually go into heat shortly after the birth. If father is in the cage, they are likely to mate. This is called back-breeding, and if kits result they will be born approximately 111 days later. If the mother is a standard chinchilla, strong and vigorous, she can manage these back-to-back pregnancies without any problem. If she is more delicate, it may be wise to remove daddy for five days or so till her time has passed, and then return him to the cage.

If you decide to let them mate make sure you have a small box or other hiding place available for the babies, so they can avoid being trampled when their parents (temporarily) forget about them.

Male Castration

If you only want one set of babies but would like mommy and daddy to be able to continue living together, you should consider getting your male chinchilla neutered. It is a fairly simple operation, but since putting a chinchilla under anesthesia is always tricky, make sure your vet has had experience carrying out this procedure with chinchillas.

As with any operation, there are some precautions you need to take to ensure a good outcome. Make sure your chinchilla is perfectly healthy and not stressed before going into the clinic or surgery. He should be well hydrated, and while it is best not to give him treats the day of the surgery, he should have had his regular food available to him.

Chapter Five: Breeding Chinchillas

Try not to bring him in much ahead of time, as the new surroundings will make him worried; arrange to not be at the veterinary office more than four hours total.

After the surgery, put him in a clean, sterile cage by himself, and make sure he has a soft bed to lie in. If you cannot clean and sterilize all of his toys and paraphernalia, you can leave some of them out until he is doing better. He should not be jumping or leaping, so either put him in a one level cage or close off the extra levels of his regular cage. Cleanliness is very important to ensure no infection sets into the new wound.

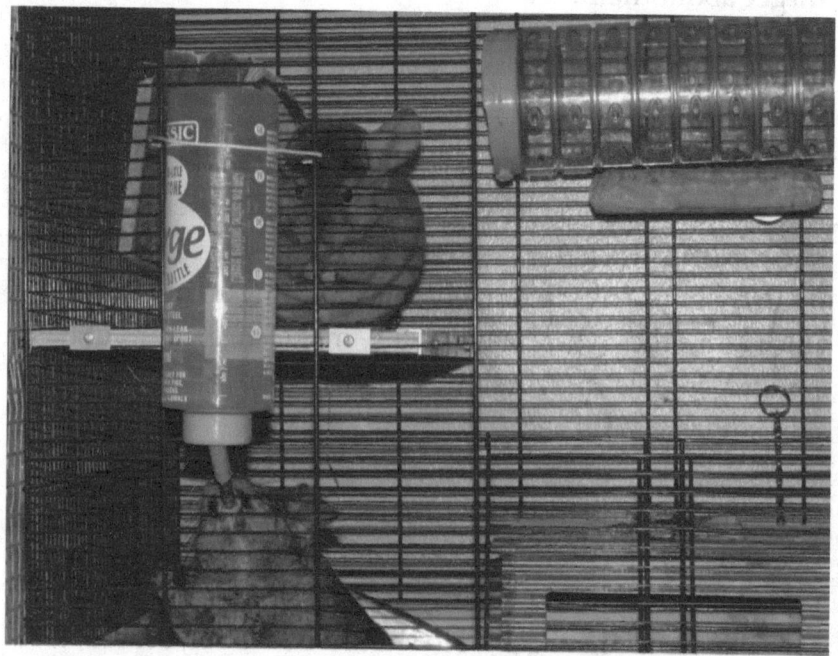

To ensure that he has peace and quiet you can cover the cage with a light cloth, and make sure it is situated in a quiet part of the house. Do keep checking up on him

Chapter Five: Breeding Chinchillas

though, and make sure he is drinking and eating. This is very important, and if he needs encouragement to drink, you can offer him a little watered down, sugar-free cranberry juice. Adding probiotic to the water in his sipper will help keep his digestive system in order.

Do not try to examine him for the first 48 hours, and give him every opportunity to rest. You can talk to your vet about giving him a painkiller such as Metacam for the first week after surgery. Painkillers reduce suffering and therefore reduce stress, thereby accelerating your chinchilla's recovery.

If he is not eating or drinking you will need to give him liquid food with a syringe. This is important, for a refusal to eat that lasts more than twenty-four hours can lead to intestinal stasis and a shutting down of the digestive system. Get a recovery diet from your vet, and follow the directions in the chapter on *Chinchilla Maintenance* in the section on refusal to eat.

After forty-eight hours have a look at the operation site. Check for redness, swelling, or any uncleanness around the stitches. If there is any problem, call up the vet office. The beginnings of any infection will need to be treated promptly with antibiotics.

You can expect your chinchilla to be nearly back to normal by about two weeks, but keep encouraging him to take it easy: it will take three months for his insides to heal completely. He can take dust baths after two weeks have

Chapter Five: Breeding Chinchillas

passed, but you should wait at least eight weeks post-surgery before introducing him again to females.

Raising the Babies

Raising the Babies with Mother in Command

When all goes well and mother is fulfilling her role your primary job is simply to make sure the cage is safe, provide benevolent oversight, and make friends with the young ones. During the first few days there may be some disruptions and squabbling as the young ones figure out how things work and establish a pecking order, but it should settle down soon.

You should weigh your kits daily. It is normal for kits to lose a little weight; as much as two to three grams (0.07-0.1 ounces) on the first and possibly second day, but after that you should see a steady uphill climb in weight, averaging about two grams (0.07 ounces) a day.

If a kit continues to lose weight or is not gaining, you should give supplemental goat milk feeds as per the directions under hand feeding below. These feedings should be in addition to, not instead of, regular feedings from mom.

If there seems to be a lot of fighting between siblings and the smaller ones are getting the short end of the stick you can also initiate rotations so they get some just-mom time. You will need to prepare a safe warm place for those you

Chapter Five: Breeding Chinchillas

are taking out; a baby-proof chinchilla carrier will be fine. Take a warm hot bottle, cover it with fleece, and place it so that it covers half or a third of the cage. You can place your larger kits here for up to two hours at a time. If they are out for two hours, make sure they have a full two hours with mom before taking them out again.

After a week or so the kits will begin eating a small amount of solid food, and you should make sure that little extra is provided. They will continue nursing until at least eight weeks, while the amount of solids they eat gradually increases. You should keep them with the mother until she has fully weaned them. Ideally father will be there too, for chinchilla kits learn a lot from both mom and dad.

You should handle the kits daily so they become used to human touch. Take them out of the cage and spend some time holding, petting and stroking them. If you let them play, make sure it is in a place where there are no little places they could hide under. They are tiny and can fit almost anywhere, and if they get under the fridge or behind the heavy couch, it will be a big job to get them out unharmed.

After the kits are ten weeks old or so you will need to separate brothers and sisters from each other and from their parents, to avoid mating between them. A pair of sisters or a pair of brothers can continue living together.

Chapter Five: Breeding Chinchillas

Plan B: How to Bring Up the Little Ones by Hand

Usually your mother chinchilla will do a fine job raising her own children. Sometimes, however, hard things happen. Your mother chinchilla may die during childbirth. She may be doing too poorly after the birth to attend to her children at all, or there may be one kit in a larger litter that she seems to be systematically ignoring.

If you are doing a larger breeding operation with a number of chinchillas you may be able to farm off the young ones to another mother. This is preferable because chinchilla milk is the ideal food for chinchilla kits, and cannot be commercially replaced. In most cases, though, it is up to you to play surrogate mother.

The best substitute for chinchilla milk is goat milk, which you can often get in powdered form. If goat milk is not available then cat milk is a close second, and is often available from a pet store or directly from your vet. If it is a powder, make it up according to the directions, with water that has been boiled and cooled so that it just barely feels warm to the skin.

You can get colostrum tablets from a pharmacy. Colostrum is the first high-vitamin substance produced by any nursing mammal, and opening a capsule and adding a small pinch of the powdered colostrum to the substitute milk will enrich it immensely.

You will need to feed your kit with a small (1 ml) syringe, with the needle removed. A medicine dropper will also do,

Chapter Five: Breeding Chinchillas

but make sure the milk is not coming out too fast and choking your nursling. Hold the kit in one hand and give the milk with the other. Start by just putting one tiny drop on your kit's lip and leave it there; the kit will lick it off, and then you can give a second drop. Eventually it will get the hang of sucking. Feed him carefully; if it chokes and inhales the milk it will go into his lung and cause infection, and it is not likely to survive.

Give as much milk as the kit seems to want. It will not be much; 1 ml is probably as much as the hungriest newborn can manage. You will need to feed every two hours for the first two or three weeks.

A chinchilla mother stimulates her kits eliminative processes by licking them vigorously on their undersides, and you will have to fill in here too. After every feeding, take a barely warm damp cloth or a damp cotton swab and gently rub the kit's lower abdomen and bottom to stimulate his bowels and encourage him to urinate. Keep it up until you get at least a few drops of urine and some tiny droppings. While your kit may not move his bowels after every feeding, it should do it at least once every twenty-four hours.

After about three weeks you can switch your feeding schedule to every three hours, and a bit longer at night — perhaps giving an evening feed at midnight and making the next one at six in the morning. The kits will start eating solid food, but it is important they still get plenty of milk. If they are not getting the milk they need they will end up eating more solids and this is not good for them, as they

Chapter Five: Breeding Chinchillas

could potentially end up with stomach disorders. Keep providing plenty of milk up until around eight weeks when your kit will be ready to be weaned.

Remember this is only an emergency measure to be used if a mother, for whatever reason, cannot feed her own kit. If she is still able to care for it, she should be allowed to; you can take it out briefly for feedings and return it to her with a full tummy.

Chapter Six: Chinchilla Maintenance

A chinchilla will be unobtrusive about illnesses. This may be a throwback to the past, when survival depended on acting well even when one was feeling half dead. Today, though, what it means is that your chinchilla is likely to be knocking at death's door before you even know something is wrong—unless you are extremely vigilant and observant.

So pay close attention to your chinchilla, and take special note of anything out of the ordinary in its behavior. Failure to eat as usual or failure to produce the usual amount of droppings are not, as with people, unimportant peripherals: they can be the only indication that something very serious is wrong with your little animal.

There are a number of illnesses that are simple to treat with antibiotics if you catch them early, but where late can easily be too late.

Chapter Six: Chinchilla Maintenance

General Signs of Illness

Only if you know your chinchilla well and stay alert to changes in behavior and appearance you will be able to tell when it is not behaving normally. Signs of illness include:
- Warm ears or veins showing in the ears;
- Dull, watery eyes, or any discharge from the eyes;
- 25% less water consumption than usual;
- 25% less food consumption than usual;
- Listlessness; sitting quietly in the cage rather than playing as normal;
- Failure to come to the door of the cage to greet you as usual (after it has bonded and made it normal behavior);
- Abnormal irritability;
- Abnormal droppings (softer or harder than usual or in smaller quantity than the normal); and
- Refusing a normally-appreciated treat.

Any of these signs should make you stop and evaluate your chinchilla carefully. Read through the common health problems listed below and assess your chinchilla in light of them. If you still cannot figure out the problem, you may need to talk to a vet or other chinchilla expert.

Common Health Problems

Heat Stroke

Because of the extreme density of a chinchilla's thick fur coat, it has a very difficult time regulating body

Chapter Six: Chinchilla Maintenance

temperature in warm weather. Your cage should never be in direct sunlight or by a heating vent. If you live in a warm climate and your house does not have air conditioning, you should not be keeping a chinchilla. Heat stroke kills quickly.

Warning Signs and Symptoms

Your chinchilla may be panting and visibly nervous. It may be lying on its side, and its oral membranes will be bluish. It will be weak, and incapable of much exertion.

Treatment

Get it cool quickly. Place ice-packs around your chinchilla, and offer cool water to drink. Move the cage to a cold environment, or if this is impossible, cool the environment with icepacks and cold, wet towels hanging over the cage. If possible, bring it to a vet, for a possible IV and corticosteroids. Otherwise encourage it to drink a little Gatorade or Pedialyte to replenish its electrolytes.

Malocclusion

This is a disorder that may sometimes be prevented but is very, very hard to cure once it has begun. If your chinchilla's teeth, growing at 3 inches a year, are not filed down sufficiently to fit neatly into the mouth, they will begin to grow backwards, up from the roots, and into the eye sockets and jaws. If you find this disease in its early stages, you may be able to reverse some damage by providing plenty of things to chew or by having your chinchilla's teeth filed at the vet. But by the time the disease progresses into backward growth there is little that can be done and nothing to look forward to but an extremely painful death.

There is a genetic factor in malocclusion, and kits of parents who suffer from the disease are more likely to get it themselves. If you buy from a breeder, always ask about the medical history of your chinchilla's parents.

Warning Signs and Symptoms

Signs of malocclusion include drooling or slobbering, watery eyes, crying while eating, refusing food, or teeth that seem large for the mouth.

You should regularly check your chinchilla's lower lip for drooling.

Treatment

Provide your chinchilla with fiber-rich hay and with plenty of things to chew on at all times! There should always be a selection of pumice stone and wooden sticks in the cage for filing teeth on.

After the disease has begun, there is much less that can be done, although if backward growth has not yet begun the overgrowth can be filed down at your veterinary clinic. If you suspect even the beginnings of malocclusion you should arrange a head x-ray and a consultation with your vet.

Chapter Six: Chinchilla Maintenance

Diarrhea

Chinchillas have weak stomachs, and are not able to handle anything other than carefully regulated, high quality chinchilla food. They are also very susceptible to bacterial or viral stomach infections. Often you will not know exactly what caused your chinchilla's problem, but you can still treat it.

Warning Signs and Symptoms

The normally dry and hard droppings you find in the cage may change to a mushy consistency or include blood or mucus. Your chinchilla may lose interest in food, and seem to have partial paralysis or difficulty moving. It may have an obviously painful abdomen, sit in a hunched position, and have dull eyes and a rough, luster-less coat.

Treatment

The first line of treatment for stomach disorders is increasing the amount of fiber in your chinchilla's diet while decreasing the amount of concentrated foods such as pellets, and completely cutting out any grains or treats you normally serve. You should also give a probiotic, preferably with *Lactobacillus* bacteria, in the drinking water. It is important that it stays hydrated; if it will not take water, it will need to be put on IV at your veterinary clinic.

If you believe the problem could be simply stress related you can serve a tiny piece of toast burnt completely black, or a tablet of activated charcoal.

Chapter Six: Chinchilla Maintenance

If this course of treatment does not bring about any change bring your chinchilla to the vet. It may need antibiotics to combat the infections in its gut. Do not wait too long; many cases of diarrhea are fatal simply because the disease is so far progressed before the owner realizes it is enough of a problem to seek medical help.

Bloat

Next time you emit an embarrassing fart, be thankful for one thing: that you *can* fart. Many animals, such as the chinchilla, have no fool-proof mechanism for releasing gas from their intestines, and what for us simply leads to an awkward situation or uncomfortable stomach pains can mean death to them, as gas builds up with no chance of release.

Just as your own flatulence may stem from any number of causes, so can your chinchilla's. In kits, it may be insufficient bowel stimulation or wrong feeding. In adults, it could be from anything to too much alfalfa in the diet, sudden diet changes, low-quality pellets and hay or too many treats.

Warning Signs and Symptoms

Your chinchilla's abdomen will be larger than usual, and if you feel it gently with your hand, it will bear resemblance to a blown-up balloon. The chinchilla will have trouble breathing and be in obvious discomfort. It may either be lying on its side or walking a little uncomfortably.

Chapter Six: Chinchilla Maintenance

Treatment

Call your vet or bring your chinchilla to the veterinary clinic immediately. The trapped gas can be removed with a stomach tube or a special needle, and there are a number of prescription drugs that may help. If you cannot get to the vet in short order, give one drop of liquid simethicone (Mylicon Baby Gas Drops), available over the counter in pharmacies and grocery stores.

If you have no simethicone and cannot get it, mix one-quarter teaspoon of baking soda with one ounce of water, and give one drop of this to your chinchilla.

Warm compresses and gentle massages may also help decrease the pain and stress. Put a sock with half a cup of dry rice in it inside the microwave for 10 to 20 seconds, and lay your chinchilla on top of it. This should be repeated for ten to twenty minutes every 2-3 hours.

A massage should be given very gently, with small circular motions. Start from the top of the abdomen and work slowly down to the anus. Do not use pressure.

Constipation

Constipation occurs most often when your chinchilla is not getting all the roughage and fiber it needs. There are a number of other possible causes also, including stress, obesity, insufficient exercise, hairballs in the intestines, and even pregnancy.

Chapter Six: Chinchilla Maintenance

Warning Signs and Symptoms

You may notice your chinchilla straining to pass droppings, or you may notice fewer droppings when you clean the cage. Droppings may be stained with blood and will be thinner, shorter, harder and more foul-smelling than usual.

Treatment

Increase the proportion of fiber in your chinchilla's diet. Avoid treats, and increase the ratio of hay to pellets. For temporary relief, a little mineral oil can be added to the chinchilla's feed. A small amount of sauerkraut juice can also be given as a laxative.

It is important to address the problem right away, as chronic constipation can lead to twisting or blockage of the intestines.

Stomach Ulcer

Young chinchillas are especially prone to stomach ulcers, inflamed lesions or holes in the stomach's mucus membrane. They are usually caused by incorrect eating — moldy food or coarse roughage being some of the chief problem foods — although stress is also a contributing factor.

Warning Signs and Symptoms

This condition gives few warning signs, and is most often found in autopsy only after the chinchilla has died from it.

Chapter Six: Chinchilla Maintenance

However, a loss of appetite and the presence of stomach pain are big danger signals. The pain in your little animal's stomach may be so severe as to cause it to periodically roll about on the ground, searching vainly for some relief.

Treatment

Prevention is the best cure. Avoid moldy, stale, or low quality hay or pellets. Do not give your chinchilla any people food or more than a small quantity of treats. Make sure it is not under undue stress.

Once your chinchilla has an ulcer, these simple preventative measures are no longer enough to enable it to heal. After your vet does gastrointestinal testing it will probably prescribe antacids and stomach coating agents. While the stomach is healing, you need to be especially careful about your recovering chinchilla's diet and feed it only high-quality, fresh, vet-approved chinchilla food.

Seizures

Seizures in chinchillas may be caused by any number of illnesses, but sometimes an otherwise healthy chinchilla will get them as a result of overexertion, overheating, or hypoglycemia (low blood sugar).

Warning Signs and Symptoms

The chinchilla will have visible involuntary muscle spasms, after which it may collapse and look limp or dead.

Chapter Six: Chinchilla Maintenance

Treatment

Stay calm, and do not create a stressful situation which will only hurt the chinchilla more. Remove anything around the chinchilla that it could hurt itself with. If the temperature is even slightly warmer than usual, think heatstroke and work to get your animal cool. If it is not warmer than usual but it has been doing more exercise than usual it may be hypoglycemia. If the seizure lasts a long time you can give it half a raisin.

Usually a seizure will not be repeated. If it is, and it is at a regular time (such as the beginning or end of out-of-cage exercise time) suspect hypoglycemia and try to stave it off next time with another half of a raisin. If this is successful, you need look no farther. You may have to limit exercise times to twice or three times a week, though, because your chinchilla cannot have many raisins.

If a raisin makes no difference to your chinchilla you need to bring it in to a knowledgeable vet for tests.

Conjunctivitis

Conjunctivitis is an inflammation of the eye frequently seen in kits and young chinchillas. It may be caused by a bacterial infection, by a virus, or simply by foreign material such as dust particles getting in the eye.

Chapter Six: Chinchilla Maintenance

Warning Signs and Symptoms

The eyes will probably be red, blood-shot and swollen. In a bacterial infection, there will usually be a mucus-like grey, yellow, or white discharge that crusts if not cleaned off. A viral infection is more likely to have a watery discharge.

Treatment

Gently clean the area with a warm damp wash cloth. If the infection seems bacterial (i.e. if there is a pus-like discharge) give antibiotic eye-drops or ointment. Do not let your infected chinchilla have a dust bath until the infection is completely over taken.

Respiratory Infections and Pneumonia

An environment that is cold, damp, or unsanitary may contribute to bacterial infections of the respiratory tract, especially in young animals. Keep alert for any signs of breathing trouble, and quarantine all animals that have respiratory infections. A chinchilla can die from an upper respiratory infection or from pneumonia before you even realize it is in trouble.

Warning Signs and Symptoms

Your chinchilla may sneeze, have a runny nose, and have conjunctivitis (infected eyes). If the disease progresses to pneumonia, the animal will have labored breathing and thick yellow discharge from the nose. It may also lose its

Chapter Six: Chinchilla Maintenance

appetite, lose weight, be listless, depressed, and unenergetic or show a fever.

Treatment

Keep your chinchilla comfortable and soak the crusts off its nose, mouth, and eyes periodically with warm wet washcloths. Make sure its home is dry and warm, although not too warm. Keep stress levels down any way you can. If the respiratory infection is severe or shows signs of a progression to pneumonia, you should bring your pet into the vet for an antibiotic prescription.

Ringworm

So-called ringworm has nothing to do with either worms or rings, but is an infection on the skin caused by dermatophytes which are a type of skin fungus. The name is from the ring-shaped sores which appear on human victims, but you will not see those on your chinchilla.

Warning Signs and Symptoms

The infection is invisible in the first stages, while it affects the skin under the chinchilla's dense coat of hair. As it progresses, though, you will see bald patches, especially around the feet, nose, and ears. These patches will be irregular shaped or circular, and the exposed skin will be flaky, crusty, and with red edges.

Chapter Six: Chinchilla Maintenance

Treatment

Ringworm is extremely contagious both to other chinchillas and to humans, so it is very important to take every sanitary precaution. Make sure your ringworm infected chinchilla is kept separate from any other chinchillas. As the infection can be airborne, the cages of healthy and infected chinchillas should not even be close to each other.

Wash your hands very thoroughly with strong anti-bacterial soap after handling either your chinchilla or anything in the cage, and make sure you do not put anything that was in the infected cage in with your other chinchillas.

The chinchilla should be given a five to six week course of oral antifungal medication; see your vet for a prescription. For the first ten days, coat the bald spots daily with topical antifungal cream such as Lamasil AT. Put an antifungal powder into the dust bath (1 teaspoon of Tinactin foot powder per cup of dust) for at least six weeks, and change the dust regularly.

Keep the cage clean, and bleach it with a mixture of bleach and water (1:10 ratio) every week till the infection is under control. Wooden chew toys and other infected items should be thrown out.

Fractures

Your chinchilla's bones are small and delicate, and rough handling or getting a limb stuck in cage wire can easily

Chapter Six: Chinchilla Maintenance

break a bone. Make sure the floor of your cage is solid to prevent injuries, and always handle your chinchilla gently.

Treatment

If your chinchilla appears to have broken a bone, you will need to bring it into the vet to have it set. After it is set, it will begin to heal quickly. Keep the chinchilla in a small, one-level cage to limit movement until the fracture is fully healed.

Barbering (Fur Chewing)

Chinchillas who are stressed or bored will often take it out on themselves or their neighbors by fur chewing. The tendency toward this is partly genetic, but is exacerbated by stressful or boredom-inducing environments.

Warning Signs and Symptoms

The chinchilla's coat will begin to look patchy and moth-eaten, and you may see it chewing on its fur or that of its neighbor.

Treatment

There is not much that can be done with a dyed-in-the-wool fur chewer, but you can alleviate the problem by helping to reduce its stress and by providing interesting things to do instead. Make sure your cage is large enough to enable exercise, put in an exercise wheel, and take your chinchilla out for exercise daily. Keep the humidity down and make

Chapter Six: Chinchilla Maintenance

sure the room is not too warm. As mentioned previously, a dehumidifier unit is a useful option for reducing humidity and condensation.

You may also want to give your chinchilla papaya cubes or tablets to reduce the chance of intestinal blockage from the hair it is ingesting.

Refusal to Eat

Refusal to eat is not so much a sickness as a symptom of sickness. However, we are discussing it in its own section here because if a chinchilla refuses to eat for more than 24 hours it will go into gastrointestinal (GI) stasis and its digestive system will turn off. In some cases this is irreversible.

Some reasons your chinchilla might refuse to eat are tooth problems, recovery from a surgery, or the side effect of antibiotics. Sometimes it may be related to depression.

Warning Signs and Symptoms

Usually the chinchilla will eat less of its pellets, then go off them entirely and only eat treats, and finally refuse treats as well.

Treatment

You need to begin treatment as soon as your chinchilla goes off its feed. Do not substitute treats for regular food, even if your chinchilla will take them. They will not provide it with

Chapter Six: Chinchilla Maintenance

the nutrition it needs and instead will give it a whole host of stomach problems.

While you hold your chinchilla in your lap, try feeding it, with a spoon, pellets that you have softened in warm water. Do not force feed these, but put them gently in or next to the chinchilla's mouth and let it eat them up. Force feeding solid food can result in choking, and a chinchilla has no gag reflex.

If your chinchilla does not eat the softened pellets, you will need to feed it a liquid recovery diet with a syringe. Oxbow Critical Care, Essentials for Life Advanced Formula Syringe Feed, and Supreme Science Recovery are the preparations most commonly used, but you may only be able to buy them through your veterinarian.

Mix the powder with water according to the directions you have been given. There is a range of possible textures, and you can experiment with your chinchilla in order to find the one that it will take most readily. One measure of powder to two measures of water is a good starting point. Let it hydrate for a few minutes, then fill a syringe.

While you are feeding, you need to hold your chinchilla firmly. Some chinchilla owners find that it helps if their pets are wrapped firmly 'burrito-style' in a towel; other chinchillas resist any attempt at swaddling and prefer being held normally.

Lift the upper lip with the syringe tip and guide the syringe between the front teeth. Feed gently, in tiny amounts,

Chapter Six: Chinchilla Maintenance

allowing the chinchilla to swallow between bites. You do not want to squirt the preparation straight into the back of the mouth as this could cause choking.

Have a damp washcloth on hand, and wipe the chinchilla's mouth whenever there is a spill. The preparation hardens and will be uncomfortable and difficult to clean later.

Feed according to your vet's recommendations, which will be based on the specific recovery feed you have been given. A general recommendation is 10 ml every 2 hours for animals under 1.5 kg, and 20 ml every 2 hours for larger animals. It is very important it gets this regularly in order to keep its gut moving.

Chapter Six: Chinchilla Maintenance

Caring For a Sick Chinchilla

Any sick chinchilla should be kept in a cool room away from bright lights or noise. Make sure it has a cozy hidey-house that can be reached without any climbing. Food should always be regularly provided, but no treats whatsoever. Monitor the drinking water and make sure that your chinchilla is drinking an adequate amount.

Limit the amount of touching to the minimum needed in order to check its condition, make sure it is not worsening, and provide the needed medicines, food and water. A sick animal mostly wants to be left alone in peace. Make sure it has a low-stress environment. A dimly lighted, quiet room is ideal for a recovering animal.

Your Chinchilla's First Aid Kit

Just as you should always keep a few medicines and bandages at home for emergencies among the people at your house, you should have a chinchilla first aid kit too. What you keep in it will depend on how many chinchillas live at your house and whether you plan to do breeding. Even for one chinchilla, though, there are some things you want to always have at hand.

- **Neosporin** for minor cuts and other wounds.
- **1 % hydrocortisone cream** for itches.
- **Tinactin or Desenex Foot Powder** for adding into the dust bath to combat ringworm.

Chapter Six: Chinchilla Maintenance

- **Lamisil AT or similar antifungal cream** for topical use on ringworm infected skin.
- **Simethicone (Mylicon Baby Gas Drops)** for treating bloat.
- **Probiotics** for digestive problems and to add to the water anytime your chinchilla is prescribed antibiotics.
- **Powdered sulfur** for helping in the prevention of fur rot. It is anti-fungal and harmless if eaten. Use at a ratio of 2 teaspoons to 1 pound of dust.
- **Syringes** (without the needle) for hand-feeding; 1 ml and 3 ml sizes.
- **Liquid Recovery Diet** such as Oxbow Critical Care or Essentials of Life, for when your chinchilla cannot eat regular food.
- **Cotton swabs & Q-tips.**
- **Gauze bandages.**
- **Sterile dressing pads and bandages.**
- **Hot water bottle or heating pad.**
- **Instant icepacks,** or **a large block of ice in the freezer**, or both.
- **Large socks or other cloth bag** to put over icepacks, and to use for hot rice compresses (see discussion of *bloat*).
- **Hand towels**, or, preferably, **spare pieces of fleece.**
- **Small fleece blanket.**
- **Small fine scissors** (think nail scissors).
- **Rectal thermometer.**
- **Latex gloves.**
- **Wet wipes.**
- **Tweezers.**
- **Stethoscope.**

Chapter Six: Chinchilla Maintenance

- **Chinchilla carrier** for trips to the vet.

If you are breeding you should also have on hand:

- **Gram scale** for regular weighing sessions.
- **Powdered goats milk** for emergency feeds or supplementation.
- **Colostrum capsules** for emergency feeds.
- **Calcium supplements** for pregnant mothers.

Have a list of emergency numbers, including the number of an exotic vet who sees chinchillas written down in some easy-to-find place.

Vaccinating Your Chinchilla

There are currently no regular vaccines for chinchillas, and your small pet should not receive vaccines meant for other animals. Take precautions against disease by keeping your animal well-fed, well-cared for, and clean. It is a good idea to give your chinchilla an initial check-up at the veterinary office after it joins your family, and then to make it a yearly habit.

Pet Insurance

Whether or not you should buy pet insurance depends entirely on your situation. If you are unable to save money it may be a good plan to buy pet insurance so that, in an

Chapter Six: Chinchilla Maintenance

emergency, you have something to fall back on. Most pet insurance will cost around $12 a month (£8) per chinchilla.

However, this insurance will not cover any number of things, including pre-existing conditions. Even if you have an unexpected emergency, your insurance will only pay a portion of the cost. And if your chinchilla stays healthy, as most well-cared for animals do, you get nothing out of your monthly payments.

In many situations it may be wiser to open up a separate bank account and start an emergency fund there, by putting away the amount you would otherwise pay to your insurance. This way, when disaster strikes, you have ready money to fall back upon without any back-and-forth haggling with insurance agents.

Chapter Seven: Common Mistakes Owners Make

Not Providing Adequate Exercise

A healthy chinchilla is an active chinchilla. It is easy to look at this little animal and think that a cage slightly bigger than a guinea pig cage should be more than adequate. There is room for a little house there, room for a yard or play place in front of the house, and maybe even a little shelf off to the side.

Chapter Seven: Common Mistakes Owners Make

What these owners are forgetting is that, in spite of their small size, a chinchilla takes large steps. This small animal has the muscles which enable it to jump six feet in the air. Can you imagine being an acrobatic gymnast or runner, locked in a little room so small you cannot even take one full stride? That is the situation you are putting your chinchilla in, so you should not be surprised if it becomes depressed and starts exhibiting neurotic behavior.
Make your cage as large as practically possible, and make sure you let your chinchilla out regularly into a larger, chinchilla-proofed area for exercise.

Improper Diet and Too Many Treats

A chinchilla has a very delicate digestive system, and very specific fiber, protein, mineral, and vitamin needs. These can be best met with timothy hay and alfalfa-based chinchilla pellets. These little animals do not eat much, which means that even just giving a little extra of something not in their diet plan will throw things off considerably. What to you seems like just a tiny taste of something good is to their metabolic systems an overwhelming amount.

Any food you give to your chinchilla should be especially meant for these animals, high quality, and fresh.

Inadequate Preventative Care

Once your animal has gotten sick, you have an uphill row to plow. Fifty years into domestication, these little animals are not thoroughly adjusted to our modern world and

Chapter Seven: Common Mistakes Owners Make

when something goes wrong, have a very precarious hold on life. But following a few simple rules of sanitation, correct diet, proper handling and exercise will help your chinchilla to live long and happy, with a minimum of vet visits.

Lack of Attention/Lack of Mental Stimulation

A chinchilla is not suited to a hermit's life of peace and quiet meditation. Although these animals are shy and easily scared, this does not mean that they should be ignored. To keep your animal healthy, both physically and mentally, you need to interact with it daily.

If you have stopped interacting with your chinchilla because of antisocial behavior on its part, you need to rethink your own behavior. Antisocial behavior is essentially a cry for help from a confused, scared, lost-feeling animal. It means you need to spend more time focusing and loving on your pet, not less.

If you are not spending much time with your chinchilla just because your schedule is crazily busy, think of ways to get creative and mix chinchillas up in your daily schedule. If you have to read through briefs or you spend a regular chunk of time composing emails, take that with you into the chinchilla proof exercise room and let your little pet play around, beside, and on you as you work.

Take a moment to talk to it and let it know that you love it and are thinking of it every time you walk by the cage. Giving your chinchilla the time it needs is more about

Chapter Seven: Common Mistakes Owners Make

sharing life with it and allowing it to be a part of your day than it is about scheduling huge blocks of chinchilla-only time.

Inadequately Chinchilla-Proofing the Exercise Room

There are so many tragedies which stem from this mistake, often made by a first-time chinchilla owner. "I let it out to play," they will say, "And then the phone rang, and I talked for maybe ten minutes, and when I got back to the chinchilla exercise room it was behaving strangely. It died the next day. What happened?"

There are a thousand things that may have happened if the room was not adequately chinchilla proofed. It may have eaten something toxic—paint, wallpaper paste, rat poison. It may have bitten on a live-wire and been left with internal injuries. It may have had something fall on it and gotten its insides crushed. Once tragedy strikes there is no going back, so make sure you have a safe, chinchilla-proof place before you let your little animal out.

Not Handling Chinchilla Kits

They are little, fragile things. Their mother is taking good care of them, and may begin to act protective if it thinks you are going to interfere. On the whole, it seems better to leave the little guys pretty much alone, right?

This is where many first-time chinchilla breeders go wrong. Yes, mother is taking good care of them, and it should be

Chapter Seven: Common Mistakes Owners Make

allowed to. But you need to be involved too, and you need to hold and handle the little kits every day. Every single day.

Mother may be protective, but if you reach in and gently pick up one of the kits it is not going to interfere. Your having 'borrowed' her baby and left your smell on him will not hurt her relationship with the little one or make her abandon him; she will be quite as affectionate as ever when you put him back.

If you leave the kits alone they will grow up wild and afraid of people. If you make daily, gentle interactions a priority, they will grow up to know people are their friends and that you are a special one.

Keeping the Cage Too Warm

A chinchilla can only handle temperatures within a certain range. Even in comfortable, temperate weather, they use huge amounts of energy just to keep themselves cool. Can you imagine having to go through life with the densest of fur coats?

Keep a thermometer in the cage and check it regularly to make sure the temperature is within appropriate limits, between 55°F and 70°F (13°C and 22°C). Around 60°F (16°C) is preferable. If it gets too hot, do something about it immediately. Turn up the air-conditioning a notch, or, if it is winter, turn the heater down. Move the cage to a cooler

Chapter Seven: Common Mistakes Owners Make

room. In emergencies, put ice-blocks around the cage and use a fan.

Starting Off Too Fast

Many new, excited owners make the mistake of starting off way too fast and traumatizing their chinchilla. As soon as it is home, they want nothing more than to pick up their chinchilla, stroke its soft fur, and watch it leaping around the room as if it were the mountain climbing exhibit at the amusement park. Then time comes to put it back, and they have no clue what to do. They start chasing, and the chinchilla starts running. The chinchilla will almost always be faster. When they do catch it, four hours later, they have a badly traumatized chinchilla who firmly believes it lives in a cave of predators, and the chinchilla has an exhausted owner who feels he or she should never, ever let that animal out of the cage again.

Do not put your chinchilla through that. Get to know your chinchilla gradually and win its trust, as detailed in the section in this book on taming your chinchilla. It is not worth rushing it. Really.

Chapter Seven: Common Mistakes Owners Make

Scaring the Chinchilla When Catching Him

Chinchillas are extremely fast and agile, and if you two race, you will lose. That is that. Make sure that putting your chinchilla back in its cage does not depend on speed. Be gentle, use measured movements, and use strategy rather than speed and rush.

Scaring it today will have consequences for tomorrow, the next day, and many days hereafter.

Chapter Eight: Frequently Asked Questions

I held a chinchilla for just one minute, and when I put him back, my hands and clothes were full of fur. Is this normal shedding?

No, this is not normal shedding, but there is nothing wrong with the chinchilla either. What is wrong is probably the way you held him. Fur slip is a mechanism by which a chinchilla escaped from enemies in their original Andean habitat. Even today, when they are stressed, frightened, or trying to get away, they will lose their hair and you will be left with a handful of fur and a (partly) naked animal.

Fur slip is not a problem, but the causes of it are. If your chinchilla is fur slipping there is something wrong in his environment or the way it is being handled. A happy, contented animal will lose only a regular small quantity of hair as part of shedding.

I'm allergic to cats, but I heard chinchillas were hypoallergenic. Will I be okay?

Chinchillas are hypoallergenic and you are extremely unlikely to get any allergic reactions from your animal's fur, but the same cannot be said for his food, dust, and the other paraphernalia in his cage. Hay, a staple of any chinchilla's diet, is also a major culprit in asthma and other allergy problems. The dust from the dust bath will go into

Chapter Eight: Frequently Asked Questions

the air and may make it difficult to breathe. Other people get allergies from chinchilla litter, and some report a reaction to chinchilla urine. So if you have allergies, a chinchilla is not likely to be the best pet for you.

How much food should my chinchilla eat?

The amount of food your chinchilla eats will depend on its age, activity level, and any special conditions. On average, you should expect your chinchilla to eat somewhat less than a handful of hay every day and a tablespoon or two of special chinchilla pellets.

When a chinchilla has problems with overeating or obesity it is because they were fed something incorrect; a chinchilla will eat only enough pellets and hay to maintain itself at its ideal weight.

Can I vary my chinchilla's diet with fresh greens every once in a while?

No. The chinchilla's digestive system does not have the enzymes necessary to deal with fresh food, and feeding it fresh greens like spinach will result in life-threatening bloat.

Observations of chinchillas in the wild have shown that when chinchillas are given the choice between their ordinary diet of dried out herbs and branches or the same things fresh, they choose the old. To us it looks unappetizing. But this, to them, is what food is supposed to be.

Chapter Eight: Frequently Asked Questions

How do I stop my chinchilla from biting?

The best way is simply to gain and maintain your chinchilla's trust. Your chinchilla will not bite unless it is afraid or threatened.

Sometimes, gaining trust is easier said than done, especially with a rescue animal that came from a difficult home. It helps to know the danger signals so you can get out of the way before you are bitten.

A chinchilla feeling threatened will first try to run away. If this is impossible, it will stand up on its hind legs and make angry noises at you. It will try to push you away with its front paws, and if this is unsuccessful, then it will give you a gentle, warning nip. A female chinchilla may spray urine. Only after this warning will the chinchilla give a real, bloody, painful bite.

If you are bitten, do not scream, hit, or throw your chinchilla. Stay calm and stay loving, and step back quietly from the situation for a minute to tend to your bite wound.

Research has shown that chinchillas kept in small cages are much more likely to exhibit aggressive behaviors such as biting than those who have lots of room for exercise. If your chinchilla seems to be getting worse and not better about dealing with people, it is time to re-evaluate your care of it and find out what you are doing wrong.

Chapter Eight: Frequently Asked Questions

How do I stop my chinchilla from spraying urine?

Again, you need to gain your chinchilla's trust. It sprays urine because it is afraid, and it has no better way to fight the big enormous creature that is you.

So be patient. When you are sprayed, do not jump, shout, or scare the chinchilla in any way. Simply speak gently let it know that you understand it is scared but that there is nothing to be frightened of.

The urine will not hurt you; all you need to do is wash your hands or clothes to get rid of it. So do not rush to drop whatever you are doing and get a clean shirt on. A fear reaction on your part will only cement the behavior. A calm, loving manner, on the other hand, will help break down the barriers that it has erected against you in its mind.

Can I give my chinchilla a bite of cookie?

Absolutely not! One bite of your cookie will cause utter havoc with its digestive system and blood sugar levels. Chinchillas have very delicate stomachs and even one bite of cookie can give it diarrhea and a stomach upset. They are also essentially diabetic, and cannot regulate their blood sugar levels unless they are given their own natural food — dry grasses.

Chapter Eight: Frequently Asked Questions

My six year old son saw a picture of a chinchilla and fell in love. Can I buy him one?

Better not. Chinchillas are delicate, sensitive animals, and not easy for children to handle. They are not as easy to bond with as other small rodents like gerbils, and they are a lot more work.

If you do decide to buy your child a chinchilla, you will have to be with him supervising him closely every time he is with his pet, and it is you who will have to bear the brunt of the chinchilla's daily care. And you will have to do it for the next ten or twenty years. You would be better off showing him cute pictures of guinea pigs or gerbils, or offer to buy him a lizard or snake.

How do I introduce chinchillas to each other as cage mates?

Follow the recommendations in our chapter on breeding. The key is—gradually, in a carefully monitored, step by step way.

My chinchilla stopped eating. Is something wrong?

A chinchilla going off its feed is always a danger sign and should never be ignored. A chinchilla tends to hide all signs of sickness until it is too late, so a decreased appetite may be the only sign you get for many of the life-threatening illnesses.

Chapter Eight: Frequently Asked Questions

Make sure the problem is not simply extreme boredom. Spend some extra time visiting with your chinchilla, and offer it the opportunity to exercise out of its cage. But if that does not fix the problem and it still turns its little nose up at the pellets and hay, take your chinchilla to the vet.

My chinchilla gave birth to a male and female kit a few months ago. Since they are all one family, can I just let them continue to live together?

Never. Once your baby chinchillas have reached sexual maturity, they will have no moral inhibitions whatever regarding intercourse within their family, and will view their brother, sister, mother, or father as if they were a chance acquaintances. The genetic reasons against close intermarriages, however, remain pressing. Any kit born of such a union is likely to be defective. So separate your males and females, and allow only such male-female pairs to live together as are capable of producing genetically sound offspring.

Can I give my chinchilla a toilet paper roll to play with?

You may, if it does not have toxic glues or paints on it. Remember, everything that a chinchilla is given it will eat. That said, if it is a basic cardboard roll, it will consider it the best toy ever and play with it for a very long time, so it makes a good gift.

Chapter Eight: Frequently Asked Questions

Can I put some colorful baby toys around the cage to make my chinchilla's place homey?

No! Anything in your chinchilla's cage your chinchilla will eat. That includes things on the ground, strung from the walls, or hanging from the ceiling. Most toys made for human children have are of toxic plastic; even wooden ones will be coated with toxic varnishes and colors.

Rather than make the cage homey your way, make it homey for your chinchilla. Since to a chinchilla the essence of home is a barren mountainside, try to make its environment as much like that as possible. To a chinchilla, a branch of an apple tree is one of the most wonderful of toys, and far more homey than your red and yellow baby rattle.

My chinchilla quivers violently and its teeth chatter when I pick it up. Is it having a seizure?

No, quivering is a perfectly normal chinchilla response to stress, excitement, or nervousness. It is nothing to worry about, although you do want to mitigate stress. Speak gently and use smooth, fluid, measured movements when interacting with it.

Teeth chattering may mean anything from worry to contentment, and is also perfectly normal behavior.

Chapter Eight: Frequently Asked Questions

Can I let visitors hold my chinchilla?

Better not, unless they are experienced chinchilla owners. Chinchillas are fragile and high strung, and you do not want all the work you just did in taming your small pet and bonding with it to be negated in thirty seconds when it is held by someone it is afraid of.

A non-accustomed holder is liable to make two opposite mistakes—holding the chinchilla gingerly, in which case it escapes and plummets to the floor, sustaining major injuries—or, afraid of dropping it, holding it tightly, in spite of it wriggling, and breaking several ribs or giving other internal injuries.

Can my chinchilla learn to understand English?

Yes! Well, that is, it can learn to understand basic one or two syllable words that you speak to it regularly in context-rich situations. Choose the words you are going to use with your chinchilla carefully, and repeat them often under appropriate circumstances. Pretty soon you'll find it can understand you well.

A chinchilla can also glean a lot of information from the tone of your voice as you talk, so make sure that it is always gentle, loving, and encouraging.

Chapter Eight: Frequently Asked Questions

Can I take my chinchilla outside for playtime in the yard, or take it for a walk with a harness?

No, you should never bring your chinchilla outside unless you need to, and then only in a safe carrier. Never let your chinchilla roam the yard for playtime. Even a limited small-animal playpen outdoors is unhealthy for them because of the dangers of temperature fluctuations, and the sun and wind of a climate that is nothing like their own.

Harnesses are off-limits inside or out, as your chinchilla's bones are very delicate and can easily be hurt by a harness.

Appendix – Reputable Breeders

If you hope to breed chinchillas yourself or just want to make sure you have a quality animal, you will want to obtain your initial animals from reputable breeders. Here is a list of some:

In the US

- **BB Chins**, Alabama. Contact bbchins@hughes.net
- **Freedom Chins**, Cullman, Alabama. Contact freedomchinchillas@yahoo.com or visit http://www.freedomchinchillas.com/
- **AZ Chins, Arizona**. Contact Rescues@azchins.com, or visit http://www.azchins.com/
- **Majestic Chinchillas,** Arizona. Contact majesticchins@roadrunner.com
- **Chin Colores Ranch**, California. Contact chincolores@sbcglobal.net
- **Chin Niche Ranch**, California. Contact chinniche@spoiledrotten.net
- **Chinchilla Chateau**, California. Contact chinchillachateau@gmail.com or visit http://chinchillachateau.googlepages.com/
- **Dees Chinchillas, California.** Contact Gerber170@aol.com
- **4Everchins**, California. Contact summers_4everchins@yahoo.com

Appendix

- Valley View Chinchillas, California. Contact ChinRanch@aol.com or visit http://www.valleyviewchinchillas.com/
- **Chinchilla Unlimited**, Colorado. Contact Chinchillaunlimited@hotmail.com
- **Crooked Acres Chinchillas**, Connecticut. Contact crookedacreschinchillas@yahoo.com
- **Angels Chinchillas**, Delaware. Contact AngeliqueDiCieli@gmail.com or visit http://angelschins.chinchillas.org/
- **Jennifer Hodge,** Cocoa, Florida. Contact Jennifermonster@cfl.rr.com or visit http://www.chinchillarampage.com/
- **Chinchillas Galore South Florida**. Contact cgrant@stu.edu or visit http://www.chinchillasgalore.com/
- **Big Daddy's Chinchillas,** Locust Grove, Georgia. Contact bigdaddyschinchillas@gmail.com or visit http://bigdaddyschinchillas.com/
- **ABC Chinchillas,** Cary, Illinois. Contact starleomach@comcast.net
- **Sydchilla**. Augusta, Maine. Contact sydchilla@hotmail.com
- **Mystic Mosiacs**, Severn Maryland. Contact mysticmosaicschinchillas@msn.com
- **Detroit Chinchillas**, Inkster, Michigan. Contact sales@detroitchinchillas.com or visit http://www.detroitchinchillas.com/

The Chinchilla Care Guide

Appendix

- **Kansas City Chinchillas**, Missouri. Contact CathleenMarieKane@msn.com or visit http://kansas.city.chinchillas.org/
- **Bear Creek Chinchillas**, Bear Creek, North Carolina. Contact bearcreekchinchillas@yahoo.com
- **Sherry Snyder**, Ohio. Contact ssnyder@alltel.net
- **Seward Breeders**, Ohio. Contact neptune@mwweb.com
- **Shoots Chinchilla Ranch**. Contact shootschinchilla@aol.com
- **Che' Chinchillas**. Contact chepaypal@yahoo.com
- **Chenlouchins**, Oklahoma. Contact chenlouchins@chenlouchins.com
- **Chincherub**. Downington, Pennsylvania. Contact chincherub@comcast.net
- **RAZberry Chinchillas**, Tennessee. Contact razberry224@yahoo.com
- **Alice**, Texas. Contact cliff-alice@msn.com
- **Chitter Chatter Chinchillas**, Utah. Contact chitterchatterchinchillas@gmail.com
- **JoAnn**, Virginia. Contact joannfryeb1@cox.net or visit http://www.luvnchins.com/
- **Pacific Northwest Chinchillas**. Contact chinchillas@juno.com

Appendix

In the UK

- **Shaw Chinchillas,** North East of England. Contact Jacci on 01642 864 654 or email jaccishaw@yahoo.com
- **Stockton on Tees,** North East England. Contact Clare: clarejohnson954@sky.com
- **West Lothian Scotland.** Contact Jean: jeanbeardshaw@blueyonder.co.uk
- **Azure Chinchillas,** Hampshire. Visit the website: http://www.azure-chinchillas.co.uk/
- **Yorkshire Chins** Phone 07859901886/07859901886 or 01274563356 or email dab21@btinternet.com
- **Chillie Chins** in Northeast Scotland. Contact Teresa: teresamargaretmoir@hotmail.co.uk or phone: 07795461617
- **Cameron's Chinchillas.** Contact Cameron at cameron6661@hotmail.co.uk or visit: http://camchinchillas.webs.com
- **Fenland Chinchillas.** Spalding, near Peterborough, Lincolnshire. Visit http://chinchilla1.wix.com/chinchillaz
- **North East Chins.** Newcastle Upon Tyne. Visit http://northeastchins.blogspot.com/ or contact Elvin and Helen at 07711964146 (mobile) email e3_silversurfer@hotmail.com
- **Trazinahs Chillaz,** Isle of Sheppey in Kent. Visit http://www.TrazinahsChillaz.webs.com

Appendix

- **Susie's Chinchillas**, Basildon, Essex, UK. Visit: http://supersue55.tripod.com/
- **Granite City Chinchillas**, Aberdeen. Contact Wenda atwenda.barron@btopenworld.com or visit http://www.granitecitychinchillas.co.uk
- **Northeast Scotland Chinchillas** Contact Lisa at Lisa1907@msn.com
- **The Wonder of Chins**, Kent. Visit http://www.thewonderofchins.moonfruit.com
- **E. R. Crutchley.** Contact webmaster@edchinchillas.co.uk
- **Kingdom Chinchillas**, Scotland. Contact kingdomchinchillas@hotmail.com or visit http://groups.msn.com/KingdomChinchillas/homepage.msnw?pgmarket=en-gb

Index

A

alarm call · 16
alleles · **86**
allergies · 137

B

back-breeding · **101**
barbering · 122
behavior · 9, 50
birth · 95, **97**
birthing complications · **98**
biting · 139
Black Velvet · 18
bloat · 114
body temperature · 21
bonding · 61
breeder · 24
breeding · **83**
buying · 24

C

caecotrophs · 70
cage · **35**
calcium · 66
carbohydrates · 66
castration · **101**
catching · **76**
characteristics · **12**
Charcoal · 18
chewing · 81
children · 141
Chile · 5
Chincha Indians · 4
Chinchilla chinchilla · 17
Choapa Valley · 10
cleaning · 48
colostrum · 106
Communication · 15
conjunctivitis · 118
constipation · 115
cost · 29, 30
Critical Care · 124

D

degu · 28
dental care · 81
diarrhea · 113
diet · 20
domestication · 11
dominant alleles · 86
dust · 80
dust bath · 44, **79**

E

ears · **13**
Ebony · 18
exercise · **72**, 131
exercise wheel · 45
exercise wheels · **73**

Index

F

family groups · 8
feeding · 65
fiber · 66
first aid kit · 126
fleece liners · 42
flying saucer · **73**
food containers · 44
fractures · 121
fresh greens · 138
fur · 12
fur chewing · 122
fur slip · 137
fur trade · 9

G

gastrointestinal stasis · 123
genetics · **85**
goat milk · 106
granite · 46

H

habitat · **5**
hair ring · 93
handfeeding · **106**
hay · **68**
heartrate · 21
heat stroke · 110
heterozygous · 86
holding · 58
homozygous · 86
hutch · 43

K

kits · 97, **104**, 133

L

Las Chinchilles National Reserve · 10
lethal factor · 89
lifespan · 21

M

malocclusion · 111
marble tile · 46
mating · 92
minerals · 66, 67
mixed feeds · **69**
mutations · **86**

N

nipping · 54
nutrition · 66, 95

O

online classifieds · 24

P

pellets · **68**
pelvis · 91

Index

pet insurance · 128
pet store · 24
playing · 62
pneumonia · 119
postnatal care · **99**
predators · 9
pregnancy · 93
protein · 66
punnet squares · 89

Q

quivering · 143

R

raisin · 71
recessive alleles · 86
refusal to eat · 123
reproduction · 8, 90
Rescue Centres · 25
rescues · 25
respiratory infections · 119
Richard Glick · 10
ringworm · 120

S

safe woods · **82**
safety · **75**
scolding · 60
scratching · 55
seizures · 117
sexing a chinchillas · 27
shedding · **78**

shelves · 44
signs of illness · 110
simethicone · 115
SPCA · 25
Standard gray · 17
stomach ulcer · 116

T

tail · **13**
taming a chinchilla · 51
toys · 45, 46
treats · 52, **70**, 131, 140

U

unsafe woods · **82**
urine scenting · 16

V

vaccines · 128
vibrissae · *See* whiskers
Violet · 18
visitors · 144

W

water sipper · 44
whiskers · **13**
wood shavings · 41
wood treatment · 46

Photo credits

Cover photo: Courtesy of Chauses Photography

Chapter 1: Pages 4, 14 Courtesy of Chauses Photography. Page 5: Map of Chinchilla Range provided by Wikipedia http://en.wikipedia.org/wiki/Chinchilla#mediaviewer/File:Range_of_Chinchilla_lanigera_and_Chinchilla_brevicaudata.svg. Page 7: Courtesy of Qiv on Flickr; licensed under Creative Commons. Pages 8, 19: Courtesy of Gemma & Paul Marchant.

Chapter 2: Pages 22, 26, 30, 33: Courtesy of Gemma & Paul Marchant.

Chapter 3: Pages 38, 40, 47 : Courtesy of Gemma & Paul Marchant. Page 43: Courtesy of Chauses Photography.

Chapter 4: Pages 50, 54, 61, 64, 65, 71, 75, 77, 79 : Courtesy of Gemma & Paul Marchant.

Chapter 5: Pages 83, 96, 102: Courtesy of Gemma & Paul Marchant.

Chapter 6: Pages 109, 125: Courtesy of Gemma & Paul Marchant. Page 129: Courtesy of Chauses Photography.

Chapter 7: Page 130: Courtesy of Gemma & Paul Marchant.

Final Credit: Thank You Cendrine Huemer for your continued selfless support. Your finely crafted editing skills and contributions were very much appreciated.

www.ingramcontent.com/pod-product-compliance
Lightning Source LLC
Chambersburg PA
CBHW010447010526
44118CB00021B/2532